EUGENE O'NEILL

Born in New York City in 18
Eugene O'Neill spent a year a
signing on as a seaman and tra
in a sanatorium recovering fro   ...st play, *A
Wife for a Life*. In 1916 he joinec   ...ncetown Players, who
produced the first of his plays to be staged, *Bound East for Cardiff*,
as well as other early work. His Broadway debut came in 1920
with *Beyond the Horizon*, which also won him a Pulitzer Prize.

The next fourteen years saw the premieres of some twenty new
plays, including *The Emperor Jones* (1920), *Anna Christie* (1921),
which won a second Pulitzer Prize, *The Hairy Ape* (1922), *All God's
Chillun Got Wings* (1924), *Desire Under the Elms* (1924), *The Great
God Brown* (1926), *Strange Interlude* (1928), which won another
Pulitzer, *Mourning Becomes Electra* (1931), a trilogy reworking the
Oresteia, Ah! Wilderness (1933) and *Days Without End* (1933), after
which thirteen years elapsed with no new play reaching the stage,
though he continued writing. Two more plays were produced
during his lifetime: *The Iceman Cometh* in 1946, though written in
1939, and *A Moon for the Misbegotten* in 1947, though it only
reached Broadway ten years later, after his death in 1953.

Plays staged posthumously include *Long Day's Journey Into Night*
(1956), which won a fourth Pulitzer, *A Touch of the Poet* (1958)
and *More Stately Mansions* (1962). He was three times married, his
third wife, Carlotta Monterey, surviving him. In 1936 he became
the first American dramatist to win the Nobel prize for
Literature.

EUGENE O'NEILL
ANNA CHRISTIE
&
THE EMPEROR JONES

Introduction by
Christine Dymkowski

NT
ROYAL NATIONAL THEATRE
London

NICK HERN BOOKS

Anna Christie & The Emperor Jones first published in this edition in 1991 jointly by the Royal National Theatre, London, and Nick Hern Books, 14 Larden Road, W3 7ST

The Emperor Jones first published in Great Britain by Jonathan Cape in 1922

Anna Christie first published in Great Britain by Jonathan Cape in 1923

Reprinted 2007

Set in Baskerville by ℞ Tek Art Ltd,
Addiscombe, Croydon, Surrey
Printed by Biddles Ltd., King's Lynn, Norfolk

British Library Cataloguing in Publication Data
O'Neill, Eugene, *1888–1953*
  Anna Christie.
  I. Title
  812.52
  ISBN 978 1 85459 101 2

Contents

Biographical Sketch of Eugene O'Neill (1888–1953)

'Some day James O'Neill will best be known as the father of
Eugene O'Neill': so Eugene himself frequently boasted
throughout 1912. The claim struck those who heard it not with a
sense of the young man's prescience but of his presumption.
Nothing in his life so far had given any indication that in less
than a decade he would be a playwright to reckon with, shaking
up the American theatre and shaping a new American drama.
Instead, he seemed more likely to become one of the pipe-
dreamers who eternally inhabit Harry Hope's no-chance saloon in
his own *The Iceman Cometh*.

Born on 16 October 1888, to the respected and accomplished
actor James O'Neill and his wife Ella Quinlan O'Neill, Eugene
was to find his family an overwhelming force in his life and to
make it the almost constant subject of his plays. He was the
O'Neills' third son: the eldest, Jamie, had been born ten years
before; a second son, Edmund, had followed five years later. Life
was not easy for the O'Neills and their two young children; James
was already touring the country in *Monte Cristo*, the vehicle that
would spell both his financial success and his artistic defeat (he
succumbed to popular demand and played the role 4000 times
between 1883 and 1912). Ella, convent-educated and proper,
loved her husband but felt she had married beneath her; she
never took to James's theatrical life or to his theatrical friends.
However, the couple could not bear to be parted, and Ella, with
great reluctance, frequently left the children in the care of her
mother to join her husband on the road. Early in 1885, on one of
these occasions, Jamie contracted measles and disobeyed
instructions to stay away from his brother; Edmund became ill
and died.

Such family history might in another case seem irrelevant, but
it is crucial for an understanding of Eugene O'Neill and of his
work. Ella did not want any more children after Edmund's death,
but James, convinced that it would help solace her, persuaded
her to have another. The result was a family tragedy that
blighted all four lives, and not least the new baby, Eugene. In an
attempt to counteract the pain of an exceedingly difficult birth,
Ella was unwittingly precipitated into the morphine addiction

from which she would suffer for the next twenty-six years. James, Jamie, and Eugene were greatly affected by Ella's distraction and withdrawal from reality, but Jamie and Eugene endured a private hell of guilt: Jamie for inadvertently killing the brother whose loss had had such drastic consequences, and Eugene for having been born at all.

Fifteen when he learned of his mother's addiction, Eugene no longer had to fear the mental illness he had up till then suspected he would inherit; the truth, however, was worse. Although summers were spent at the family's home in New London, Connecticut, their haphazard existence in a succession of hotels while James was on tour had already given Eugene a sense of rootlessness that plagued him all his life. Now, guilty that his birth had effected such misery, he developed a deep sense of unbelonging that at times manifested itself as a death-wish. He rejected his parents' Catholicism and, under Jamie's influence, began to drink and to visit brothels. Both Jamie and Eugene, displacing their anger, blamed their father for their mother's condition, accusing him of hiring a 'quack' to attend Ella at Eugene's birth. In fact, even reputable doctors at that time prescribed morphine, and in doses so low that addiction was by no means inevitable.

Eugene entered Princeton in 1906, but only stayed a year, having spent most of his time drinking, cutting classes, and following his own reading interests. It was at this time that he discovered Nietzsche's *Thus Spake Zarathustra*, which together with the works of Strindberg, became his personal bible. After leaving Princeton, he worked for a short time in a New York office job arranged by his father. In the city's Greenwich Village, Hell's Kitchen, and Tenderloin districts, he began to frequent the dives he would immortalise in many of his plays and also began to write poetry. O'Neill remained a heavy drinker for years, though he never drank while writing; in 1926 he gave up alcohol completely, lapsing only a few times thereafter.

Wishing to escape from a romantic entanglement with Kathleen Jenkins, O'Neill let his father arrange for him to join a mining expedition in Honduras in October 1909. Nevertheless, because Kathleen was pregnant, he agreed to marry her shortly before his departure. Having contracted malaria after a few months in Central America, Eugene returned to the US and, without visiting his wife and new-born son (Eugene O'Neill, Jr.), joined his father's company on tour, checking tickets. Shortly afterwards, in June 1910, O'Neill boarded the *Charles Racine*, a Norwegian windjammer, as a working passenger on its two-month voyage to

Buenos Aires. O'Neill loved the sea – he was throughout his life a keen and able swimmer – and now had the chance to experience a sailing life first-hand; it was an experience he would exploit in many of his early plays.

O'Neill remained in Argentina for several months, occasionally working but mainly living as a down-and-out; he sailed back to New York in March 1911 on the S.S. *Ikala*, this time as a member of the crew. He stayed in New York long enough to arrange for a divorce, living in an alcoholic haze at a downtown bar and flophouse called Jimmy-the-Priest's. In July, he signed onto the S.S. *New York* as an ordinary seaman for its voyage to Southampton; he returned in August on the S.S. *Philadelphia* as an able-bodied seaman, a qualification of which he was to remain proud for the rest of his life. Resuming his destitute way of life at Jimmy-the-Priest's – though he regularly attended the performances of Dublin's Abbey Players, who were visiting New York – O'Neill sank progressively into a depression that in January 1912 culminated in a suicide attempt. When he had sufficiently recovered, he rejoined his father's company for a few months, this time taking on small acting roles.

1912 seemed to mark a watershed in O'Neill's life, as evidenced both by his boasting of future fame and by his setting of many of his most autobiographical plays in that year. Moving to New London, Connecticut, in the summer, he worked as a reporter for the *Telegraph*, continued to write poetry, and developed a mild case of tuberculosis. By the end of the year, he was at the Gaylord Farm Sanatorium, where he was to remain for six months. During that time he decided to become a playwright.

Returning to New London in summer 1913 and boarding with the Rippins, a local family, he began to write one-act plays based on his own experiences. O'Neill's father subsidised their publication as *Thirst and Other One Act Plays* in August 1914, and the following September O'Neill enrolled in Professor George Pierce Baker's famous play-writing course at Harvard. Although he did not particularly distinguish himself in the class, his disdain for easy formulaic success made clear his ambition to be an original dramatist.

After his year at Harvard, O'Neill returned to New York and became somewhat involved in the political and intellectual life of Greenwich Village, frequenting the Golden Swan saloon, familiarly known as the 'Hell Hole'. He submitted some plays to the adventurous Washington Square Players, who had recently formed in reaction to the glib, commercial offerings of Broadway; however, the Players were not so adventurous as to stage any of O'Neill's works.

His first real theatrical opportunity came in June 1916 when he accompanied his friend Terry Carlin to Provincetown, at the tip of Massachusetts's Cape Cod. Then, as now, Provincetown boasted a flourishing artists' colony each summer. The previous year, the writer Susan Glaspell, her husband Jig Cook, and other vacationing Greenwich Village friends had staged an impromptu production, marking the birth of what would become the Provincetown Players. When O'Neill arrived in Provincetown, the group were desperately short of plays for their new season. O'Neill offered them *Bound East for Cardiff*, which premiered on 28 July 1916, the first-ever performance of an O'Neill play. His work with the Players also led to his involvement in Greenwich Village's radical circle, which included John Reed, Louise Bryant, Mabel Dodge, and Floyd Dell, among others.

The Provincetown Players' success was such that in September 1916 they moved operations to Greenwich Village, acquiring a base on Macdougal Street, which at O'Neill's suggestion was named the Playwrights' Theatre. During the group's eight subscription seasons between 1916 and 1922, O'Neill had ample opportunity to experiment without regard to commercial considerations. For example, *The Emperor Jones*, staged by the Provincetown Players in November 1920, not only had an African-American for its protagonist but was also considerably shorter than standard length. Despite its unconventionality, the play marked the group's first popular success: following its scheduled performances at the Playwrights' Theatre, it moved uptown to Broadway for an unlimited run. When the original Provincetown Players disbanded, O'Neill, together with the designer Robert Edmond Jones and the critic-producer Kenneth Macgowan, founded the Experimental Theatre, Inc., in 1923. The triumvirate ran the Playwrights' Theatre, now renamed the Provincetown Playhouse, from 1923–25 and the Greenwich Village Theatre from 1924–26.

The Provincetown Players' success with *The Emperor Jones* was not O'Neill's first theatrical triumph. *Beyond the Horizon*, which opened at the Morosco Theatre on Broadway in February 1920, was greeted by extremely favourable reviews, transferred for an extended run, and brought O'Neill his first Pulitzer Prize (the second drama award in the prize's four year history). This success was quickly followed by another: *Anna Christie* opened in November 1921 and brought him a second Pulitzer. He was to win the award twice more, for *Strange Interlude* in 1928 and posthumously in 1956 for *Long Day's Journey into Night*, a record that has not been matched.

By the time of his early success, O'Neill's personal life had undergone considerable change: married for a second time, to the writer Agnes Boulton, he had become a father again with the birth of Shane Rudraighe O'Neill on 30 October 1919 (his last child, Oona, who later married Charlie Chaplin, was born on 14 May 1925). His father had died in August 1920, having lived long enough to see his younger son succeed; in the year prior to his death, Eugene had finally recognised his father's long-standing forbearance and support and had become friendly with him. Ironically, O'Neill's own neediness so dominated his life that he could never be a father to his own children, who all suffered the neglect for which O'Neill had bitterly and unfairly resented his own father. Eugene Jr. committed suicide at the age of forty, and Shane was for many years a heroin addict.

Within three years of his father's death, O'Neill was the sole survivor of his original family: his mother died of a brain tumour in February 1922, and Jamie had drunk himself to death by November 1923. Their deaths freed O'Neill to explore the dark side of his family life, which he proceeded to do in plays as diverse (and variously successful) as *All God's Chillun Got Wings*, *Dynamo*, *Long Day's Journey Into Night*, and *A Moon for the Misbegotten*. Further change was in store: in 1927 O'Neill left Agnes Boulton for Carlotta Monterey, who became his third wife in July 1929. Misogynist, desirous of a mother, unable to separate love from hate, O'Neill had difficult relationships with women. He found his own guilt at his desertion of Agnes too difficult to deal with, and, as he later did with his children, manufactured grievances against her. His third marriage fulfilled his desire that his wife should be completely dedicated to his own interests, but it was a stormy one with cruelty on both sides.

O'Neill was quintessentially an autobiographical playwright; many of his protagonists are recognisable O'Neill figures, sharing the playwright's own lean build and dark deep-set eyes. All of his experiences found their way onto the stage, from the sea-going life depicted in early one-act plays like *Bound East for Cardiff* to his ambivalence about parenthood in *The First Man* to his Strindbergian view of marital relations in *Welded*. This need to depict, explain, and justify himself had considerable ramifications for his role as a playwright: he could not really regard theatre as the collaborative activity it so patently is. Time and again, O'Neill lamented the process of staging his plays, complaining that the ideal play he had seen in his head never existed in production. Whereas playwrights generally welcome the new life that actors and directors bring to their work, O'Neill saw it as a betrayal. So strongly did he feel this that he virtually never went to any productions of his plays, only attending rehearsals in order to advise and to cut when necessary.

In addition, his personal investment in what he wrote often blinded him to its deficiencies: he could be convinced that inferior works like *Welded*, *Dynamo*, and *Days Without End* were undervalued and misjudged. For example, while *Dynamo* ostensibly focused on the relationship between humankind, machines, and religion, it was really O'Neill's working out of his ambivalent relationship to his mother: small wonder that it made more sense to O'Neill than to the critics. However, at his best, O'Neill was able to transmute his personal experiences into the most powerful of dramas, as he does in works like *Long Day's Journey into Night* and *The Iceman Cometh*.

Although he wrote essentially to please himself and to exorcise his private demons (as early as 1924 he claimed that 'Writing is my vacation from living'), O'Neill was genuinely interested in stretching American drama beyond the narrow confines it had so far inhabited. His experiments were many: trying to make the audience share a character's hallucination in *Where the Cross is Made*, extending the audience's endurance by writing four- and five-hour long plays, using set location schematically in *Beyond the Horizon*, incorporating expressionistic elements in *The Hairy Ape*, masking the characters in *The Great God Brown*, modernising the use of the aside in *Strange Interlude*, developing a modern equivalent for the Greek sense of tragedy in *Desire Under the Elms* and *Mourning Becomes Electra*, creating an ambitious play-cycle detailing a critical history of America through the story of one family in *A Tale of Possessors Self-Dispossessed* (of which only *A Touch of the Poet* was completed to his satisfaction).

Although his achievements won him the Nobel prize for literature in 1936, in the last years of his life O'Neill was something of a has-been. He had suffered for years from a hand tremor, caused by a rare degenerative disease of the cerebellum that attacks the motor system, which made writing increasingly difficult; by 1943, it had become impossible. Since O'Neill had never been able to compose at a typewriter or by dictation, his writing career, apart from some revisions, was effectively over. Furthermore, he was extremely depressed by the Second World War: it made his writing seem of little consequence and the staging of his work even less important and appropriate. Consequently, he refused to authorise productions of new plays; none appeared between *Days Without End* in 1933 and *The Iceman*

Cometh in 1946. When the latter was finally staged, the inadequate production did little to restore interest in O'Neill's work.

Throughout his life, O'Neill had roamed far in search of a home and a sense of belonging: New York, Connecticut, Provincetown, Bermuda, France, Georgia, California. Sometime before his death on 27 November 1953, O'Neill struggled up from his bed to complain 'I knew it, I knew it! Born in a goddam hotel room and dying in a hotel room!' Only with the posthumous revival of *The Iceman Cometh* and the first production of *Long Day's Journey into Night* in 1956 did his reputation, like his life, come full circle.

Christine Dymkowski
Lecturer in Drama and Theatre Studies
Royal Holloway and Bedford New College
University of London

Introduction to the Plays

Anna Christie and *The Emperor Jones*, which O'Neill wrote during
1919–20, were two of his earliest successes. He had made notes
on *Chris Christopherson*, the play that was to become *Anna Christie*,
in summer 1918, returning to it again in early 1919. The finished
play, now called *Chris*, was optioned by George C. Tyler, an old
associate of his father's, and in March 1920, with Lynn Fontanne
as Anna, it was tried out in Atlantic City, N.J., and Philadelphia,
Pa., where it closed after 19 performances. The character of
Chris in this version is similar to that in *Anna Christie*, but his
daughter is an English-educated typist and the sailor she falls in
love with an American, college-educated second mate. O'Neill
realised that he had developed Chris's character at the expense of
the two lovers and, despite several attempts to revise the script,
finally abandoned it altogether.

After his father's death on 10 August 1920, O'Neill entered an
intensely creative period: returning to *Chris* after the funeral, he
finished the new version on 18 September, calling it first *The Ole
Davil* and then *Anna Christie*. In mid-September he began work
on a new play, *The Silver Bullet*, which he finished on 2 October
and renamed *The Emperor Jones*. By 19 October he had completed
yet another play, *Diff'rent*.

As with all of O'Neill's work, these plays contain many
autobiographical elements. 'Johnny-the-Priest's', the saloon of
Anna Christie's Act 1, and its eponymous bartender were modelled
on O'Neill's Fulton Street hang-out, Jimmy-the-Priest's, and its
owner. Chris Christopherson was similarly taken from life,
complete with name, occupation, and attitude to 'dat ole davil'
sea, though his real-life counterpart regularly returned to
Norway to see his wife and six children. Mat Burke owed
something of his character to O'Neill's stoker friend Driscoll of
the S.S. *Philadelphia*, while Anna drew some of her history from
Marie, a former prostitute who had lived with his friend Terry
Carlin; she also resembled Christine Ell, one of O'Neill's
Greenwich Village set. Anna's response to the sea obviously
reflects O'Neill's own positive experience of it, while his time in
Central America helped him to imagine the jungle of *The Emperor
Jones*. Jones himself was partly drawn from some of O'Neill's

African-American friends: Adam Scott was an elder of the
Baptist Church in New London, Connecticut, who in his
bartending job expressed sentiments similar to Jones's 'I lays my
Jesus on de shelf for de time bein''.

Both plays also contain elements drawn from anecdotes, books,
and current theatrical trends. For example, from a circus friend
who had toured the West Indies, O'Neill had heard a story about
the Haitian president Vilbrun Guillaume Sam: Sam had
purportedly boasted that if he were ever overthrown he would
not let himself fall into his enemies' hands but would kill himself
with a silver bullet; a lead one was not special enough. *The
Emperor Jones* was further influenced by Gordon Craig's *The
Theatre Advancing*, which he had read earlier in the year, and by
Joseph Conrad's *Heart of Darkness*; Sheaffer points out that
O'Neill's play reflects Craig's advocacy of masks, dance, and
pantomime and shares Conrad's depiction of oppressive woods,
monotonous drumbeats, and personal disintegration (*Son and
Artist*, p. 28). In addition, Travis Bogard convincingly details
many similarities between the play and Ibsen's *Peer Gynt* (*Contour
in Time*, p. 136). European experiments in expressionism, as well
as Jung's theory of the collective unconscious, were further
influences on the play. The motivating force of *Anna Christie*'s
plot, 'the woman with a past', had become a stage convention
long before O'Neill began to write. While such a character was
most often doomed to an unhappy end, plays like Shaw's *Mrs
Warren's Profession* (1894) had already overturned such audience
expectations.

The Emperor Jones was the first of the two plays to reach the
stage; directed by Jig Cook, it premiered at the Playwrights'
Theater on 1 November 1920. The production was ground-
breaking in several regards. The title role was played by Charles
S. Gilpin, the first time in America that a black actor had ever
had a significant part in a play staged by a white company; usual
practice would have cast a white actor in black make-up as Brutus
Jones. Cook also insisted that O'Neill's varied settings could only
be contained within a sky dome, a plan rejected by the
Provincetown Players because of its prohibitive expense. Taking
unilateral action, Cook built the dome himself with cement, iron
bars, and steel netting. Similar domes had been used in Europe,
but this was the first to appear on an American stage. A quarter
section of a sphere occupying eight feet of the stage depth, the
dome when lit was able to provide an illusion of immense
distance, thus justifying its monopoly of the limited stage space
available at the Playwrights' Theater.

The Emperor Jones was a resounding success for the Provincetown Players, one that would ironically lead to their demise. Audiences flocked to the box office wanting to become members in order to see the play; contrary to usual practice, its run was extended at the Playwrights' Theater. On 27 December the whole production was moved uptown to the Selwyn Theater, transferring again to the Princess Theater on 29 January 1921; in all, 204 performances were given in New York before the play's two seasons on the road. The long run sidetracked the Players from their original aims, and the payment of salaries interfered with collective work: within two years the group had disbanded.

Much of the play's success was due to Gilpin's masterly portrayal of Brutus Jones. Heywood Broun, writing in the *Tribune* (4 November 1920), called it 'the most thrilling performance we have seen any place this season' and emphasised its skill: 'there can be no question whatever that in *The Emperor Jones* Gilpin is great'. Alexander Woollcott, for the *New York Times* (7 November 1920), agreed that it was an 'uncommonly powerful and imaginative performance'. Both critics complained of the long waits between scene changes which dissipated attention, and both admired the play itself. Woollcott also commented on the 'heightening effect' of the tom-tom which grew nearer and faster as the play progressed, 'an ominous accompaniment to [Jones's] mounting panic'; O'Neill's stage directions stipulate that the beat should start at 72 to the minute to correspond to the normal pulse and should increase its rate at regular intervals until Jones is killed.

Gilpin's performance managed to please the harshest critic of all, O'Neill himself. Notoriously unsatisfied by most attempts to embody characters whose every feature he had already outlined in minutest detail, O'Neill on this occasion had nothing but praise. Only three actors were ever to satisfy him and only Gilpin did so completely: 'I can honestly say', O'Neill revealed in 1946, 'there was only one actor who carried out every notion of a character I had in mind. That actor was Charles Gilpin . . .' (*New York Times*, 15 September 1946). However, O'Neill's attitude to Gilpin soured during the run of *The Emperor Jones* as the actor began to change some of the playwright's offensive language, for example substituting other words for 'nigger'. O'Neill also complained that Gilpin was drinking too much during the 1922/23 season to give an effective performance. O'Neill consequently refused to let him play the part when the production went to London, preferring to see it taken by Paul Robeson, who appeared as Jones in a 1924 revival at the Provincetown

Playhouse and in the 1933 film version directed by Dudley Murphy. Gilpin, however, again played the part in two different 1926 revivals in New York.

Anna Christie reached the stage a year later than The Emperor Jones, opening at the Vanderbilt Theater on 2 November 1921. After the Theater Guild had decided against a co-production of the play, Tyler allowed his option on it to expire. It was taken up by Arthur Hopkins, one of the best and most progressive of American directors at the time, who chose to produce only those plays he believed in. Pauline Lord was engaged to play Anna, with George Marion as Chris and Frank Shannon as Mat, while Robert Edmond Jones, Hopkins's usual collaborator, designed the scenery.

Although the play was a tremendous hit, running for 177 performances and earning its author his second Pulitzer Prize, O'Neill was upset by its reception. Many of the critics commented on the happy ending the play seemed to suggest, an ending that O'Neill was adamant he had not written. Some critics also implied that in providing such a conclusion O'Neill had finally learned to take popular taste into account, a charge that further infuriated him. It is unclear whether O'Neill misjudged the effect of the ending or whether Hopkins contrived to make it more positive, but the author was moved enough to write to the New York Times to make his purpose clear: he complained that 'a kiss in the last act, a word about marriage, and the audience grows blind and deaf to what follows' (18 December 1921).

O'Neill had already taken steps to avoid such a response. The critic George Jean Nathan, to whom he had sent the play for comment earlier that year, had also judged the conclusion a happy one. O'Neill had replied in a letter that he once thought of calling the play Comma, since 'The happy ending is merely the comma at the end of a gaudy introductory clause, with the body of the sentence still unwritten' (1 February 1921). He added that he would negate the misleading impression he had created by having 'the stoker not entirely convinced by the oath of a non-Catholic . . .', but this change failed to have the desired effect and only added to the comedy. Despite the critical acclaim heaped on the play, O'Neill grew to despise it, refusing to include it in a selection of his plays published in 1932. It was several times made into a motion picture, first as a 1923 silent version starring Blanche Sweet and later as Greta Garbo's first 'talkie' in 1930.

The New York productions of both plays transferred to London, with Anna Christie arriving earlier. The first West End production of an O'Neill play, it opened at the Strand Theatre on

10 April 1923 to a 'wildly demonstrative' audience (*Daily Mail*, 11 April 1923): Pauline Lord took a dozen curtain calls after Act 3, the act in which she confronts Chris and Mat with her past (*The Times*, 11 April 1923). While most critics judged Lord's performance magnificent (e.g., *The Times*, *Daily Telegraph*, and *Observer*), Sydney W. Carroll felt her success in the part more due to O'Neill's writing than her own acting (*Sunday Times*, 15 April 1923). St. John Ervine, however, felt he had no hope of ever seeing great acting if this were not it: Lord acted with her whole body, almost the first time he had ever witnessed such a portrayal (*Observer*, 15 April 1923). The *Daily Telegraph* underlined his point, commenting on Lord's use of body language to contrast the tired Anna of the first act with the later rejuvenated Anna.

The play went on to have a long run of 103 performances, with critical reaction similar to that in New York. While American reviewers had generally hailed the play, their praise had been mixed with criticism. The *Herald*, for example, had felt the play was too long, while Woollcott, although regarding it as the best play in town, had decided it was not first-rate O'Neill: Chris became rather tedious in performance and much of the play was dross. In London, the same mixture of kudos and minor reservations prevailed. The fourth act was regarded as unconvincing (*Daily Mail*, *Morning Post*, *The Times*, *Observer*), though *The Times* found it skilful. While several reviewers commented on the way O'Neill had made living people out of stock characters (*Daily Mail*, *Daily Telegraph*), others were not so happy with the characterisation of Mat Burke. Both Carroll and Ervine saw him as drawn from Synge, a point that had been also made less negatively by the *New York Tribune*. Ervine saw him as a 'literary convention', not a living person: 'Mat Burke is the Playboy of the Western World after he has taken to drink and become a Sinn Fein gunman'. Ervine found his language derived from Christy Mahon (the Playboy), and the drinking reconciliation between him and Chris reminiscent of the ending of *The Shadow of the Glen*. However, despite his reservations about O'Neill's theatrically contrived depiction of Mat, happy ending, excess of speech, and careless handling of material, Ervine judged *Anna Christie* a 'very fine play'. Carroll regarded it as 'almost, but not quite, a masterpiece' (*Sunday Times*).

The Emperor Jones opened at the Ambassadors' Theatre, London, on 10 September 1925 in a production by James Light, who had joined the Provincetown Players in 1917 (Jig Cook, the original director, had died in 1924). The cast, different from that of the first New York production, included Paul Robeson as

Brutus Jones, S. Victor Stanley as Harry Smithers, and Irene Howe as the old woman. Robeson attracted excellent notices, though St. John Ervine's comment – that he appeared 'too intellectual' for the part – reflected the feelings of New York critics who had measured his performance against Gilpin's (*Observer*, 13 September 1925). The play itself received a mixed press. The *Morning Post* reviewer enjoyed the first scene but was disappointed in the rest, finding that performance accentuated a monotony of structure that was less noticeable when the play was read. Ervine also found the play too repetitious, and that the effect of the gun-shot to end Jones's phantom encounters palled with its five occurrences; in addition, he found the beating of the tom-tom, which carried on right through the intervals, an irritating attempt to involve the audience in the protagonist's emotion. Nevertheless, he judged *The Emperor Jones* a 'remarkable' play which should be seen. His view was echoed by the critic of *The Times*, who found the drumming effective.

James Agate, writing for the *Sunday Times* (13 September 1925), was less impressed. While he joined in the praise for Robeson's 'wonderful' acting, he had far more reservations about the play itself. He judged its closing scenes less actable on account of its material: he was unable to believe in Jones's dreams and found the crocodile god too reminiscent of *Peter Pan*'s Captain Hook. More importantly, one of his comments raises the question of the play's inherent racism: Agate's approving view that Robeson's presence made it hard for an audience member to theorise white supremacy suggests that such an attitude is indeed implicit in the play. The fact that Ervine's review described Jones's 'reversion to type' supports this contention, as does O'Neill's description of Lem as an 'ape-faced old savage of the extreme African type'. While *The Emperor Jones* had an undeniable role in making white American audiences take black actors seriously, it did not itself break down stereotypes: in fact, like *Heart of Darkness*, it helped to validate them.

Both plays would seem to have limited attractions for a modern audience, but recent London revivals attest otherwise. For instance, reviews of Stuart Wood's production of *The Emperor Jones* at the Offstage Downstage Theatre in Camden Town, which opened on 17 January 1991, show that modern sensitivities view the racial aspect of the play in different ways: while some critics were embarrassed by the patronising dialect given to Jones, others saw the play as a condemnation of white 'civilisation'. In addition, it is still viewed as a bold theatrical experiment, offering great opportunities as well as dangers to designer and director.

David Thacker's production of *Anna Christie* at the Young Vic, which opened on 14 June 1990, was greeted with rapturous critical acclaim and popular success: although the creaking melodrama of the plot does not escape attention, reviews show that the force of Anna Christie's character and her feminist stand in Act 3 can keep the play alive for a contemporary audience.

Christine Dymkowski
March 1991

Sources

Bogard, Travis. *Contour in time: The Plays of Eugene O'Neill.* Revised ed. New York: Oxford University Press, 1988.

Bogard, Travis and Jackson R. Breyer, eds. *Selected Letters of Eugene O'Neill.* New Haven and London: Yale University Press, 1988.

Cargill, Oscar, et al., eds. *O'Neill and His Plays: Four Decades of Criticism.* New York: New York University Press, 1961.

Floyd, Virginia, ed. *Eugene O'Neill at Work: Newly Released Ideas for Plays.* New York: Frederick Ungar, 1981.

Gelb, Arthur and Barbara. *O'Neill.* New York: Harper, 1960.

Miller, Jordan Y. *Eugene O'Neill and the American Critic: A Summary and Bibliographical Checklist.* Second edition, revised. Hamden, Connecticut: Archon, 1973.

Ranald, Margaret Loftus. *The Eugene O'Neill Companion.* Westport, Conn., and London: Greenwood, 1984.

Sheaffer, Louis. *O'Neill: Son and Playwright.* London: Dent, 1968.

——————. *O'Neill: Son and Artist.* London: Paul Elek, 1973.

Wainscott, Ronald H. *Staging O'Neill: The Experimental Years, 1920–1934.* New Haven and London: Yale University Press, 1988.

I would also like to thank Sue Cusworth of RHBNC and Janet Birkett of the Theatre Museum for help in tracing British productions of O'Neill's plays.

List of O'Neill's Produced Plays

Title	Year Written*	First Production	First London Production
The Web	1913–14	39th Street Theatre, New York 17 March 1924	
Thirst	1913–14	Wharf Theatre, Provincetown, Mass. Summer 1916	
Fog	1913–14	Playwrights' Theater, New York 5 January 1917	
Bound East for Cardiff	1913–14	Wharf Theatre, Provincetown, Mass. 28 July 1916	(see *S.S. Glencairn*)
Servitude	1913–14	Skylark Theatre N.Y. International Airport 22 April 1960	
Abortion	1913–14	Key Theatre, New York 27 October 1959	
The Movie Man	1914	Key Theatre, New York 27 October 1959	

Title	Year Written*	First Production	First London Production
The Sniper	1915	Playwright's Theater, New York 16 February 1917	
Before Breakfast	1916	Playwrights' Theater, New York 1 December 1916	Gate Theatre 30 August 1926
Ile	1916–17	Playwrights' Theater, New York 30 November 1917	Everyman Theatre 17 April 1922
In the Zone	1916–17	Comedy Theater, New York (Washington Square Players) 31 October 1917	Everyman Theatre 15 June 1921
The Long Voyage Home	1916–17	Playwrights' Theater, New York 2 November 1917	Everyman Theatre 12 June 1925
The Moon of The Caribbees	1916–17	Playwrights' Theater, New York 20 December 1918	(see S.S. Glencairn)

Play	Year	American premiere	British premiere
S.S. Glencairn (*Bound East for Cardiff, In the Zone, Moon of the Caribbees,* and *Long Voyage Home*)		Barnstormer's Barn Provincetown, Massachusetts 14 August 1924	Mercury Theatre 9 June 1947
The Rope	1918	Playwrights' Theater, New York 26 April 1918	
The Dreamy Kid	1918	Playwrights' Theater, New York 31 October 1919	(Festival Theatre, Cambridge 14 May 1928)
Beyond the Horizon	1918	Morosco Theater, New York 3 February 1920	Regent Theatre (The Repertory Players) 31 January 1926
Where the Cross is Made	1918	Playwrights' Theater, New York 22 November 1918	Arts Theatre 27 October 1927
The Straw	1918–19	Greenwich Village Theater, New York 10 November 1921 (after an out-of-town try-out)	
Exorcism	1919	Playwrights' Theater, New York 26 March 1920	

Title	Year Written*	First Production	First London Production
Chris (1st version of *Anna Christie*)	1919	Apollo Theater, Atlantic City, N.J. 8 March 1920	
Gold	1920	Frazee Theater, New York 1 June 1921	
Anna Christie	1920	Vanderbilt Theater, New York 2 November 1921	Strand Theatre 10 April 1923
The Emperor Jones	1920	Playwrights' Theater, New York 1 November 1920	Ambassadors' Theatre 10 September 1925
Diff'rent	1920	Playwrights' Theater, New York 27 December 1920	Everyman Theatre 4 October 1921
The First Man	1921	Neighborhood Playhouse, New York 4 March 1922	
The Hairy Ape	1921	Playwrights' Theater, New York 9 March 1922	
The Fountain	1921–22	Greenwich Village Theater, New York 10 December 1925	Gate Theatre 26 January 1928

Welded	1922–23	39th Street Theater, New York 17 March 1924	The Playroom Six 16 February 1928
All God's Chillun Got Wings	1923	Provincetown Playhouse, New York 15 May 1924	Gate Theatre 8 November 1926
The Ancient Mariner (adaptation)	1924	Provincetown Playhouse (previously Playwrights' Theater), New York 6 April 1924	
Desire Under The Elms	1924	Greenwich Village Theater, New York 11 November 1924	Gate Theatre 24 February 1931
Marco Millions	1923–25	Guild Theater, New York 9 January 1928	Westminster Theatre 26 December 1938 (also produced at Festival Theatre, Cambridge, 1932)
The Great God Brown	1925	Greenwich Village Theater, New York 23 January 1926	Strand Theatre (Stage Society) 19 June 1927
Lazarus Laughed	1925–26	Pasadena Community Playhouse, California 9 April 1928	

Title	Year Written*	First Production	First London Production
Strange Interlude	1926–27	John Golden Theater, New York 30 January 1928	Lyric Theatre 3 February 1931
Dynamo	1928	Martin Beck Theater, New York 11 February 1929	
Mourning Becomes Electra	1929–31	Guild Theater, New York 26 October 1931	Westminster Theatre 19 November 1937
Ah, Wilderness!	1932	Nixon Theater, Pittsburgh, Pennsylvania 25 September 1933 (out-of-town tryout before New York opening at Guild Theater, 2 October 1933)	Westminster Theatre 4 May 1936
Days Without End	1932–33	Plymouth Theater, Boston, Mass. 27 December 1933 (out-of-town tryout before New York opening at Guild Theater, 8 January 1934)	Grafton Theatre (Stage Society) 3 February 1935

A Touch of the Poet	1935–42	Royal Dramatic Theatre, Stockholm, Sweden 29 March 1957 (first American production at Helen Hayes Theater, New York, 2 October 1958)	Young Vic Theatre 20 January 1988 (also produced at Ashcroft Theatre, Croydon, 16 September 1963)
More Stately Mansions	1936–42	Royal Dramatic Theatre, Stockholm, Sweden 11 September 1962 (first American production at Ahmanson Theater, Los Angeles, California, 12 November 1967)	Greenwich Theatre 19 September 1974
The Iceman Cometh	1939	Martin Beck Theater, New York 9 October 1946	Arts Theatre 29 January 1958
Long Day's Journey into Night	1939–41	Royal Dramatic Theatre, Stockholm, Sweden 10 February 1956 (first American production at Helen Hayes Theater, New York, 7 November 1956)	Globe Theatre 24 September 1958 (transfer from Lyceum Theatre, Edinburgh, 8 September 1958)
Hughie	1941–42	Royal Dramatic Theatre, Stockholm, Sweden 18 September 1958	Duchess Theatre 18 June 1963
A Moon for the Misbegotten	1943	Hartman Theater, Columbus, Ohio (Guild Theater production) 20 February 1947	Arts Theatre 20 January 1960

*Dates of composition are approximate.

ANNA CHRISTIE

Characters

'JOHNNY-THE-PRIEST'
TWO LONGSHOREMEN
A POSTMAN
LARRY, Bar-tender
CHRIS CHRISTOPHERSON, Captain of the barge *Simeon Winthrop*
MARTHY OWEN
ANNA CHRISTOPHERSON, CHRIS's daughter
THREE MEN OF A STEAMER'S CREW
MAT BURKE, a Stoker
JOHNSON, Deckhand on the barge

Scenes

ACT ONE

'Johnny-the-Priest's' saloon near the water-front, New York City

ACT TWO

The barge, *Simeon Winthrop*, at anchor in the harbour of Provincetown, Mass. Ten days later

ACT THREE

Cabin of the barge, at dock in Boston. A week later

ACT FOUR

The same. Two days later

Time of the Play – About 1910

ACT ONE

'Johnny-the-Priest's' saloon near South Street, New York City. The stage is divided into two sections, showing a small back room on the right. On the left, forward, of the bar-room, a large window looking out on the street. Beyond it, the main entrance – a double swinging door. Farther back, another window. The bar runs from left to right nearly the whole length of the rear wall. In back of the bar, a small showcase displaying a few bottles of goods, for which there is evidently little call. The remainder of the rear space in front of the large mirrors is occupied by half-barrels of cheap whisky of the 'nickel-a-shot' variety, from which the liquor is drawn by means of spigots. On the right is an open doorway leading to the back room. In the back room are four round wooden tables with five chairs grouped about each. In the rear, a family entrance opening on a side street.

It is late afternoon of a day in autumn.

As the curtain rises, JOHNNY *is discovered.* 'JOHNNY-THE-PRIEST' *deserves his nickname. With his pale, thin, clean-shaven face, mild blue eyes, and white hair, a cassock would seem more suited to him than the apron he wears. Neither his voice nor his general manner dispels this illusion which has made him a personage of the water-front. They are soft and bland. But beneath all his mildness one senses the man behind the mask – cynical, callous, hard as nails. He is lounging at ease behind the bar, a pair of spectacles on his nose, reading an evening paper.*

Two longshoremen enter from the street, wearing their working aprons, the button of the Union pinned conspicuously on the caps pulled sideways on their heads at an aggressive angle.

FIRST LONGSHOREMAN (*as they range themselves at the bar*).
Gimme a shock. Number Two. (*He tosses a coin on the bar.*)

SECOND LONGSHOREMAN. Same here.

JOHNNY *sets two glasses of barrel whisky before them.*

FIRST LONGSHOREMAN. Here's luck!

The other nods. They gulp down their whisky.

SECOND LONGSHOREMAN (*putting money on the bar*). Give us another.

FIRST LONGSHOREMAN. Gimme a scoop this time – lager and porter. I'm dry.

SECOND LONGSHOREMAN. Same here.

JOHNNY *draws the lager and porter and sets the big, foaming tankards before them. They drink down half the contents and start to talk together hurriedly in low tones. The door on the left is swung open and* LARRY *enters. He is a boyish, red-cheeked, rather good-looking young fellow of twenty or so.*

LARRY (*nodding to* JOHNNY – *cheerily*). Hallo, boss!

JOHNNY. Hallo, Larry! (*With a glance at his watch.*) Just on time.

LARRY *goes to the right, behind the bar, takes off his coat, and puts on an apron.*

FIRST LONGSHOREMAN (*abruptly*). Let's drink up and get back to it.

They finish their drinks and go out left. THE POSTMAN *enters as they leave. He exchanges nods with* JOHNNY *and throws a letter on the bar.*

THE POSTMAN. Addressed care of you, Johnny. Know him?

JOHNNY *picks up the letter, adjusting his spectacles.* LARRY *comes and peers over his shoulder.* JOHNNY *reads very slowly.* Christopher Christopherson.

THE POSTMAN (*helpfully*). Square-head name.

LARRY. Old Chris – that's who.

JOHNNY. Oh, sure. I was forgetting Chris carried a hell of a name like that. Letters come here for him sometimes before, I remember now. Long time ago, though.

THE POSTMAN. It'll get him all right, then?

JOHNNY. Sure thing. He comes here whenever he's in port.

THE POSTMAN (*turning to go*). Sailor, eh?

JOHNNY (*with a grin*). Captain of a coal barge.

THE POSTMAN (*laughing*). Some job! Well, s'long.

JOHNNY. S'long. I'll see he gets it. (THE POSTMAN *goes out.* JOHNNY *scrutinizes the letter.*) You got good eyes, Larry. Where's it from?

LARRY (*after a glance*). St Paul. That'll be in Minnesota, I'm thinkin'. Looks like a woman's writing too, the old divil!

JOHNNY. He's got a daughter somewheres out West, I think he told me once. (*He puts the letter on the cash register.*) Come to think of it, I ain't seen old Chris in a dog's age. (*Putting his overcoat on, he comes around the end of the bar.*) Guess I'll be gettin' home. See you tomorrow.

LARRY. Good night to ye, boss.

As JOHNNY *goes toward the street door, it is pushed open and* CHRISTOPHER CHRISTOPHERSON *enters. He is a short, squat, broad-shouldered man of about fifty, with a round, weather-beaten, red face from which his light-blue eyes peer short-sightedly, twinkling with a simple good humour. His large mouth, overhung by a thick, drooping, yellow moustache, is childishly self-willed and weak, of an obstinate kindliness. A thick neck is jammed like a post into the heavy trunk of his body. His arms, with their big, hairy, freckled hands, and his stumpy legs terminating in large, flat feet, are awkardly short and muscular. He walks with a clumsy, rolling gait. His voice, when not raised in a hollow boom, is toned down to a sly, confidential half-whisper with something vaguely plaintive in its quality. He is dressed in a wrinkled, ill-fitting, dark suit of shore clothes, and wears a faded cap of grey cloth over his mop of grizzled, blond hair. Just now his face beams with a too-blissful happiness, and he has evidently been drinking. He reaches his hand out to* JOHNNY.

CHRIS. Hallo, Yohnny! Have drink on me. Come on, Larry. Give us a drink. Have one yourself. (*Putting his hand in his pocket.*) Ay gat money – plenty money.

JOHNNY (*shakes* CHRIS *by the hand*). Speak of the devil. We was just talkin' about you.

LARRY (*coming to the end of the bar*). Hallo, Chris! Put it there. (*They shake hands.*)

CHRIS (*beaming*). Give us drink.

JOHNNY (*with a grin*). You got a half-snootful now. Where'd you get it?

CHRIS (*grinning*). Oder fallar on oder barge – Irish fallar – he gat bottle vhisky and we drank it, yust us two. Dot vhisky get kick, by yingo! Ay yust come ashore. Give us drink, Larry, Ay vas little drunk, not much. Yust feel good. (*He laughs and commences to sing in a nasal, high-pitched quaver.*)
    'My Yosephine, come board de ship. Long time Ay vait for
        you.
    De moon, she shi-i-i-ine. She looka yust like you.
    Tchee-tchee, tchee-tchee, tchee-tchee, tchee-tchee.'

To the accompaniment of this last he waves his hand as if he were conducting an orchestra.

JOHNNY (*with a laugh*). Same old Yosie, eh, Chris?

CHRIS. You don't know good song when you hear him. Italian fallar on oder barge, he learn me dat. Give us drink. (*He throws change on the bar.*)

LARRY (*with a professional air*). What's your pleasure, gentlemen?

JOHNNY. Small beer, Larry.

CHRIS. Vhisky – Number Two.

LARRY (*as he gets their drinks*). I'll take a cigar on you.

CHRIS (*lifting his glass*). Skoal! (*He drinks.*)

JOHNNY. Drink hearty.

CHRIS (*immediately*). Have oder drink.

JOHNNY. No. some other time. Got to go home now. So you've just landed? Where are you in from this time?

CHRIS. Norfolk. Ve make slow voyage – dirty vedder – yust fog, fog, fog, all bloody time! (*There is an insistent ring from the doorbell at the family entrance in the back room. CHRIS gives a start – hurriedly.*) Ay go open, Larry. Ay forgat. It vas Marthy. She come with me. (*He goes into the back room.*)

LARRY (*with a chuckle*). He's still got that same cow livin' with him, the old fool!

JOHNNY (*with a grin*). A sport, Chris is. Well, I'll beat it home. S'long (*He goes to the street door.*)

LARRY. So long, boss.

JOHNNY. Oh – don't forget to give him his letter.

LARRY. I won't.

JOHNNY *goes out. In the meantime, CHRIS has opened the family entrance door, admitting MARTHY. She might be forty or fifty. Her jowly, mottled face, with its thick, red nose, is streaked with interlacing purple veins. Her thick, grey hair is piled anyhow in a greasy mop on top of her round head. Her figure is flabby and fat; her breath comes in wheezy gasps; she speaks in a loud, mannish voice, punctuated by explosions of hoarse laughter. But there still twinkles in her bloodshot blue eyes a youthful lust for life which hard usage has failed to stifle, a sense of humour, mocking, but good-tempered. She wears a man's cap, double-breasted man's jacket, and a grimy, calico skirt. Her bare feet are encased in a man's shoes several sizes too large for her, which gives her a shuffling, wobbly gait.*

MARTHY (*grumblingly*). What yuh tryin' to do, Dutchy – keep me standin' out there all day? (*She comes forward and sits at the table in the right corner, front.*)

CHRIS (*mollifyingly*). Ay'm sorry, Marthy. Ay talk to Yohnny. Ay forgat. What you goin' take for drink?

MARTHY (*appeased*). Gimme a scoop of lager an' ale.

CHRIS. Ay go bring him back. (*He returns to the bar.*) Lager and ale for Marthy, Larry. Vhisky for me. (*He throws change on the bar.*)

LARRY. Right you are. (*Then remembering, he takes the letter from in back of the bar.*) Here's a letter for you – from St Paul, Minnesota – and a lady's writin'. (*He grins.*)

CHRIS (*quickly – taking it*). Oh, den it come from my daughter, Anna. She live dere. (*He turns the letter over in his hands uncertainly.*) Ay don't gat letter from Anna – must be a year.

LARRY (*jokingly*). That's a fine fairy tale to be tellin' – your daughter! Sure, I'll bet it's some tart.

CHRIS (*soberly*). No. Dis come from Anna. (*Engrossed by the letter in his hand – uncertainly.*) By golly, Ay tank Ay'm too drunk for read dis letter from Anna. Ay tank Ay sat down for a minute. You bring drinks in back room, Larry. (*He goes into the room on right.*)

MARTHY (*angrily*). Where's my lager an' ale, yuh big stiff?

CHRIS (*preoccupied*). Larry bring him.

He sits down opposite her. LARRY brings in the drinks and sets them on the table. He and MARTHY exchange nods of recognition. LARRY stands looking at CHRIS curiously. MARTHY takes a long draught of her tankard and heaves a huge sigh of satisfaction, wiping her mouth with the back of her hand. CHRIS stares at the letter for a moment – slowly opens it, and squinting his eyes, commences to read laboriously, his lips moving as he spells out the words. As he reads his face lights up with an expression of mingled joy and bewilderment.

LARRY. Good news?

MARTHY (*her curiosity also aroused*). What's that yuh got – a letter, fur Gawd's sake?

CHRIS (*pauses for a moment, after finishing the letter, as if to let the news sink in – then suddenly pounds his fist on the table with happy excitement*). Py yiminy! Yust tank, Anna say she's comin' here right avay! She gat sick on yob in St Paul, she say. It's short letter, don't tal me much more'n dat. (*Beaming.*) Py golly, dat's good news all at one time for ole fallar! (*Then turning to* MARTHY, *rather shamefacedly.*) You know, Marthy, Av've tole you Av don't see my Anna since she vas little gel in Sveden five year ole.

MARTHY. How old'll she be now?

CHRIS. She must be – lat me see – she must be twenty year ole, py Yo!

LARRY (*surprised*). You've not seen her in fifteen years?

CHRIS (*suddenly growing sombre – in a low tone*). No. Ven she vas little gel, Av vas bo'sun on vindyammer. Av never gat home only few time dem year. Ay'm fool sailor fallar. My voman – Anna's mother – she gat tired vait all time Sveden for me ven Av don't never come. She come dis country, bring Anna, dey go out Minnesota, live with her cousins on farm. Den ven her mo'der die ven Ay vas on voyage, Ay tank it's better dem cousins keep Anna. Ay tank it's better Anna live on farm, den she don't know dat ole davil, sea, she don't know fader like me.

LARRY (*with a wink at* MARTHY). This girl, now'll be marryin' a sailor herself, likely. It's in the blood.

CHRIS (*suddenly springing to his feet and smashing his fist on the table in a rage*). No, py God! She don't do dat!

MARTHY (*grasping her tankard hastily – angrily*). Hey, look out, yuh nut! Wanta spill my suds for me?

LARRY (*amazed*). Oho, what's up with you? Ain't you a sailor yourself now, and always been?

CHRIS (*slowly*). Dat's yust vhy Av say it. (*Forcing a smile.*) Sailor vas all right fallar, but not for marry gel. No. Ay know dat. Anna's mo'der, she know it, too.

LARRY (*as* CHRIS *remains sunk in gloomy reflection*). When is your daughter comin'? Soon?

CHRIS (*roused*). Py yiminy, Ay forgat. (*Reads through the letter hurriedly.*) She say she come right avay, dat's all.

LARRY. She'll maybe be comin' here to look for you, I s'pose. *He returns to the bar, whistling. Left alone with* MARTHY, *who stares at him with a twinkle of malicious humour in her eyes,* CHRIS *suddenly becomes desperately ill at ease. He fidgets, then gets up hurriedly.*

CHRIS. Ay gat speak with Larry. Ay be right back (*Mollifyingly.*) Ay bring you oder drink.

MARTHY (*emptying her glass*). Sure. That's me. (*As he retreats with the glass she guffaws after him derisively.*)

CHRIS (*to* LARRY *in an alarmed whisper*). Py yingo, Ay gat gat Marthy shore off barge before Anna come! Anna raise hell if she find dat out. Marthy raise hell, too, for go, py golly!

LARRY (*with a chuckle*). Serve ye right, ye old divil – havin' a woman at your age!
CHRIS (*scratching his head in a quandary*). You tal me lie for tal Marthy, Larry, so's she gat off barge quick.

LARRY. She knows your daughter's comin'. Tell her to get the hell out of it.

CHRIS. No. Ay don't like make her feel bad.

LARRY. You're an old mush! Keep your girl away from the barge, then. She'll likely want to stay ashore, anyway. (*Curiously.*) What does she work at, your Anna?

CHRIS. She stay on dem cousins' farm till two year ago. Dan she gat yob nurse gel in St Paul (*Then shaking his head resolutely.*) But Ay don't vant for her gat yob now. Ay vant for her stay with me.

LARRY (*scornfully*). On a coal barge! She'll not like that, I'm thinkin'.

MARTHY (*shouts from next room*). Don't I get that bucket o'suds, Dutchy?

CHRIS (*startled – in apprehensive confusion*). Yes, Ay come, Marthy.

LARRY (*drawing the lager and ale, hands it to* CHRIS – *laughing*). Now you're in for it! You'd better tell her straight to get out!

CHRIS (*shaking in his boots*). Py golly. (*He takes her drink in to* MARTHY *and sits down at the table. She sips it in silence.* LARRY *moves quietly close to the partition to listen, grinning with expectation.* CHRIS *seems on the verge of speaking, hesitates, gulps down his whisky desperately as if seeking for courage. He attempts to whistle a* few bars of 'Yosephine' with careless bravado, but the whistle peters out futilely. MARTHY stares at him keenly, taking in his embarrassment with a malicious twinkle of amusement in her eye. CHRIS clears his throat.) Marthy –

MARTHY (aggressively). Wha's that? (Then, pretending to fly into a rage, her eyes enjoying CHRIS's misery.) I'm wise to what's in back of your nut, Dutchy. Yuh want to get rid o' me, huh? – now she's comin'. Gimme the rush ashore, huh? Lemme tell yuh, Dutchy, there ain't a square-head workin' on a boat man enough to git away with that. Don't start nothin' yuh can't finish!

CHRIS (miserably). Ay don't start nutting, Marthy.

MARTHY (glares at him for a second – then cannot control a burst of laughter). Ho-ho! Yuh're a scream, Square-head – an honest-ter-Gawd knock-out! Ho-ho! (She wheezes, panting for breath.)

CHRIS (with childish pique). Ay don't see nutting for laugh at.

MARTHY. Take a slant in the mirror and yuh'll see. Ho-ho! (Recovering from her mirth – chuckling, scornfully.) A square-head tryin' to kid Marthy Owen at this late day – after me campin' with barge-men the last twenty years. I'm wise to the game, up, down, and sideways. I ain't been born and dragged up on the water-front for nothin'. Think I'd make trouble, huh? Not me! I'll pack up me duds an' beat it. I'm quittin' yuh, get me? I'm tellin' yuh I'm sick of stickin' with yuh, and I'm leavin' yuh flat, see? There's plenty of other guys on other barges waitin' for me. Always was, I always found. (She claps the astonished CHRIS on the back.) So cheer up, Dutchy! I'll offen the barge before she comes. You'll be rid o'me for good – and me o'you – good riddance for both of us. Ho-ho!

CHRIS (seriously). Ay don' tank dat. You vas good gel, Marthy.

MARTHY (grinning). Good girl? Aw, can the bull! Well, yuh treated me square, yuhself. So it's fifty-fifty. Nobody's sore at nobody. We're still good frien's, huh?

LARRY returns to bar.

CHRIS (beaming now that he sees his troubles disappearing). Yes, py golly.

MARTHY. That's the talkin'! In all my time I tried never to split with a guy with no hard feelin's. But what was yuh so scared about – that I'd kick up a row? That ain't Marthy's way. (Scornfully.) Think I'd break my heart to loose yuh? Commit

suicide, huh? Ho-ho! Gawd! The world's full o'men if that's all
I'd worry about! (*Then with a grin, after emptying her glass.*) Blow
me to another scoop, huh? I'll drink your kid's health for yuh.

CHRIS (*eagerly*). Sure tang. Ay go gat him. (*He takes the two glasses
into the bar.*) Oder drink. Same for both.

LARRY (*getting the drinks and putting them on the bar*). She's not
such a bad lot, that one.

CHRIS (*jovially*). She's good gel, Ay tal you! Py golly, Ay calabrate
now! Give me vhisky here at bar, too. (*He puts down money.
LARRY serves him.*) You have drink, Larry?

LARRY (*virtuously*). You know I never touch it.

CHRIS. You don't know what you miss. Skoal! (*He drinks – then
begins to sing loudly.*)
    'My Yosephine, come board me ship –'
(*He picks up the drinks for MARTHY and himself and walks unsteadily into the back room, singing.*)
    'De moon she shi-i-i-ine, She looks yust like you.
    Tchee-tchee, tchee-tchee, tchee-tchee, tchee-tchee.'

MARTHY (*grinning, hands to ears*). Gawd!

CHRIS (*sitting down*). Ay'm good singer, yes? Ve drink, eh? Skoal!
Ay calabrate! (*He drinks.*) Ay calabrate 'cause Anna's coming
home. You know, Marthy, Ay never write for her to come,
'cause Ay tank Ay'm no good for her. But all time Ay hope like
hell some day she vant for see me and den she come. And dat's
vay it happen now, py yiminy! (*His face beaming.*) What you tank
she look like, Marthy? Ay bet you she's fine, good, strong gel,
pooty like hell! Living on farm made her like dat. And Ay bet
you some day she marry good, steady land fallar her in East,
have home all her own, have kits – and dan Ay'm ole
grandfader, py golly! And Ay go visit dem every time Ay gat in
port near! (*Bursting with joy.*) By yiminy crickens, Ay calabrate
dat! (*Shouts.*) Bring oder drink, Larry! (*He smashes his fist on the
table with a bang.*)

LARRY (*coming in from bar – irritably*). Easy there! Don't be
breakin' the table, you old goat!

CHRIS (*by way of reply, grins foolishly and begins to sing*). 'My
Yosephine comes board de ship –'

MARTHY (*touching CHRIS's arm persuasively*). You're soused to
the ears, Dutchy. Go out and put a feed into you. It'll sober

you up. (*Then as* CHRIS *shakes his head obstinately.*) Listen, yuh old nut! Yuh don't know what time your kid's liable to show up. Yuh want to be sober when she comes, don't yuh?

CHRIS (*aroused – gets unsteadily to his feet*). Py golly, yes.

LARRY. That's good sense for you. A good beef stew'll fix you. Go round the corner.

CHRIS. All right. Ay be back soon, Marthy. (CHRIS *goes through the bar and out the street door.*)

LARRY. He'll come round all right with some grub in him.

MARTHY. Sure.

LARRY *goes back to the bar and resumes his newspaper.* MARTHY *sips what is left of her tankard reflectively. There is the ring of the family entrance bell.* LARRY *comes to the door and opens it a trifle – then, with a puzzled expression, pulls it wide.*

ANNA CHRISTOPHERSON *enters. She is a tall, blonde, fully developed girl of twenty, handsome after a large, Viking-daughter fashion, but now run down in health and plainly showing all the outward evidences of belonging to the world's oldest profession. Her youthful face is already hard and cynical beneath its layer of make-up. Her clothes are the tawdry finery of peasant stock turned prostitute. She comes and sinks wearily in a chair by the table, left front.*

ANNA. Gimme a whisky – ginger ale on the side. (*Then, as* LARRY *turns to go, forcing a winning smile at him.*) And don't be stingy, baby.

LARRY (*sarcastically*). Shall I serve it in a pail?

ANNA (*with a hard laugh*). That suits me down to the ground. (LARRY *goes into the bar. The two women size each other up with frank stares.* LARRY *comes back with the drink, which he sets before* ANNA, *and returns to the bar again.* ANNA *downs her drink at a gulp. Then, after a moment, as the alcohol begins to rouse her, she turns to* MARTHY *with a friendly smile.*) Gee, I needed that bad, all right, all right!

MARTHY (*nodding her head sympathetically*). Sure – yuh look all in. Been on a bat?

ANNA. No – travelling – day and a half on the train. Had to sit up all night in the dirty coach too. Gawd, I thought I'd never get here!

MARTHY (*with a start – looking at her intently*). Where'd yuh come from, huh?

ANNA. St Paul – out in Minnesota.

MARTHY (*staring at her in amazement – slowly*). So – yuh're – (*She suddenly bursts out into hoarse, ironical laughter.*) Gawd!

ANNA. All the way from Minnesota, sure. (*Flaring up.*) What you laughing at? Me?

MARTHY (*hastily*). No, honest, kid. I was thinkin' of somethin' else.

ANNA (*mollified – with a smile*). Well, I wouldn't blame you, at that. Guess I do look rotten – yust out of the hospital two weeks. I'm going to have another 'ski. What d'you say? Have something on me?

MARTHY. Sure I will. T'anks. (*She calls.*) Hey, Larry! Little service!

LARRY *comes in.*

ANNA. Same for me.

MARTHY. Same here.

LARRY *takes their glasses and goes out.*

ANNA. Why don't you come sit over here, be sociable. I'm a dead stranger in this burg – and I ain't spoke a word with no one since day before yesterday.

MARTHY. Sure thing.

She shuffles over to ANNA*'s table and sits down opposite her.* LARRY *brings the drinks and* ANNA *pays him.*

ANNA. Skoal! Here's how! (*She drinks.*)

MARTHY. Here's luck! (*She takes a gulp from her tankard.*)

ANNA (*taking a package of Sweet Caporal cigarettes from her bag*). Let you smoke in here, won't they?

MARTHY (*doubtfully*). Sure (*Then with evident anxiety.*) On'y trow it away if yuh hear some one comin'.

ANNA (*lighting one and taking a deep inhale*). Gee, they're fussy in this dump, ain't they? (*She puffs, staring at the table top.* MARTHY *looks her over with a new penetrating interest, taking in every detail of her face.* ANNA *suddenly becomes conscious of this appraising stare – resentfully.*) Ain't nothing wrong with me, is there? You're looking hard enough.

MARTHY (*irritated by the other's tone – scornfully*). Ain't got to look much. I got your number the minute you stepped in the door.

ANNA (*her eyes narrowing*). Ain't you smart! Well, I got yours, too, without no trouble. You're me forty years from now. That's you! (*She gives a hard little laugh.*)

MARTHY (*angrily*). Is that so? Well, I'll tell you straight, kiddo, that Marthy Owen never – (*She catches herself up short – with a grin.*) What are you and me scrappin' over? Let's cut it out, huh? Me, I don't want no hard feelin's with no one. (*Extending her hand.*) Shake and forget it, huh?

ANNA (*shakes her hand gladly*). Only too glad to. I ain't looking for trouble. Let's have 'nother. What d'you say?

MARTHY (*shaking her head*). Not for mine. I'm full up. And you – had anythin' to eat lately?

ANNA. Not since this morning on the train.

MARTHY. Then yuh better go easy on it, hadn't yuh?

ANNA (*after a moment's hesitation*). Guess you're right. I got to meet some one, too. But my nerves is on edge after that rotten trip.

MARTHY. Yuh said yuh was just outa the hospital?

ANNA. Two weeks ago. (*Leaning over to* MARTHY *confidentially.*) The joint I was in out in St Paul got raided. That was the start. The judge give all us girls thirty days. The others didn't seem to mind being in the cooler much. Some of 'em was used to it. But me, I couldn't stand it. It got my goat right – couldn't eat or sleep or nothing. I never could stand being caged up nowheres. I got good and sick and they had to send me to the hospital. It was nice there. I was sorry to leave it, honest!

MARTHY (*after a slight pause*). Did yuh say yuh got to meet some one here?

ANNA. Yes. Oh, not what you mean. It's my Old Man I got to meet. Honest! It's funny, too. I ain't seen him since I was a kid – don't even know what he looks like – yust had a letter every now and then. This was always the only address he give me to write him back. He's yanitor of some building here now – used to be a sailor.

MARTHY (*astonished*). Janitor!

ANNA. Sure. And I was thinking maybe, seeing he ain't never done a thing for me in my life, he might be willing to stake me to a room and eats till I get rested up. (*Wearily.*) Gee, I sure need that rest! I'm knocked out. (*Then resignedly.*) But I ain't expecting much from him. Give you a kick when you're down that's what all men do. (*With sudden passion.*) Men, I hate 'em – all of 'em! And I don't expect he'll turn out no better than the rest. (*Then with sudden interest.*) Say, do you hang out around this dump much?

MARTHY. Oh, off and on.

ANNA. Then maybe you know him – my Old Man – or at least seen him?

MARTHY. It ain't old Chris, is it?

ANNA. Old Chris?

MARTHY. Chris Christopherson, his full name is.

ANNA (*excitedly*). Yes, that's him! Anna Christopherson – that's my real name – only out there I called myself Anna Christie. So you know him, eh?

MARTHY (*evasively*). Seen him about for years.

ANNA. Say, what's he like, tell me – honest?

MARTHY. Oh, he's short and –

ANNA (*impatiently*). I don't care what he looks like. What kind is he?

MARTHY (*earnestly*). Well, yuh can bet your life, kid, he's as good an old guy as ever walked on two feet. That goes!

ANNA (*pleased*). I'm glad to hear it. Then you thinks he'll stake me to that rest cure I'm after?

MARTHY (*emphatically*). Surest thing you know. (*Disgustedly.*) But where'd yuh get the idea he was a janitor?

ANNA. He wrote me he was himself.

MARTHY. Well he was lyin'. He ain't. He's captain of a barge – five men under him.

ANNA (*disgusted in her turn*). A barge? What kind of a barge?

MARTHY. Coal, mostly.

ANNA. A coal barge! (*With a harsh laugh.*) If that ain't a swell job to find your long-lost Old Man working at! Gee, I knew something'd be bound to turn out wrong – always does with me. That puts my idea of his giving me a rest up the spout.

MARTHY. What d'yuh mean?

ANNA. I s'pose he lives on the boat, don't he?

MARTHY. Sure. What about it? Can't you live on it, too?

ANNA (scornfully). Me? On a dirty coal barge! What d'you think I am?

MARTHY (resentfully). What d'yuh know about barges, huh? Bet yuh ain't never seen one. That's what comes of his bringing yuh up inland – away from the old divil sea – where yuh'd be safe – Gawd! (The irony of it strikes her sense of humour and she laughs hoarsely.)

ANNA (angrily). His bringing me up! Is that what he tells people! I like his nerve! He let them cousins of my Old Woman's keep me on their farm and work me to death like a dog.

MARTHY. Well, he's got queer notions on some things. I've heard him say a farm was the best place for a kid.

ANNA. Sure. That's what he'd always answer back – and a lot of crazy stuff about staying away from the sea – stuff I couldn't make head or tail to. I thought he must be nutty.

MARTHY. He is on that one point. (Casually.) So yuh didn't fall for life on the farm, huh?

ANNA. I should say not! The old man of the family, his wife, and four sons – I had to slave for all of 'em. I was only a poor relation, and they treated me worse than they dare treat a hired girl. (After a moment's hesitation – sombrely.) It was one of the sons – the youngest – started me – when I was sixteen. After that, I hated 'em so I'd killed 'em all if I'd stayed. So I run away – to St Paul.

MARTHY (who has been listening sympathetically). I've heard Old Chris talkin' about your bein' a nurse girl out there. Was that all a bluff yuh put up when yuh wrote him?

ANNA. Not on your life, it wasn't. It was true for two years. I didn't go wrong all at one jump. Being a nurse girl was yust what finished me. Taking care of other people's kids, always listening to their bawling and crying, caged in, when you're only a kid yourself and want to go out and see things. At last I got the chance – to get into that house. And you bet your life I took it! (Defiantly.) And I ain't sorry neither. (After a pause – with

bitter hatred.) It was all men's fault – the whole business. It was
men on the farm ordering and beating me – and giving me the
wrong start. Then when I was a nurse, it was men again
hanging around, bothering me, trying to see what they could
get. (*She gives a hard laugh.*) And now it's men all the time.
Gawd, I hate 'em all, every mother's son of 'em! Don't you?

MARTHY. Oh, I dunno. There's good ones and bad ones, kid.
You've just had a run of bad luck with 'em, that's all. Your Old
Man, now – old Chris – he's a good one.

ANNA (*sceptically*). He'll have to show me.

MARTHY. Yuh kept right on writing him yuh was a nurse girl
still, even after yuh was in the house, didn't yuh?

ANNA. Sure (*Cynically.*) Not that I think he'd care a darn.

MARTHY. Yuh're all wrong about him, kid. (*Earnestly.*) I know
Old Chris well for a long time. He's talked to me 'bout you lots
o' times. He thinks the world o' you, honest he does.

ANNA. Aw, quit the kiddin'!

MARTHY. Honest! Only, he's a simple old guy, see? He's got
nutty notions. But he means well, honest. Listen to me, kid –
(*She is interrupted by the opening and shutting of the street door in the
bar and by hearing* CHRIS's *voice.*) Ssshh!

ANNA. What's up?

CHRIS (*who has entered the bar. He seems considerably sobered up*). Py
golly, Larry, dat grub taste good. Marthy in back?

LARRY. Sure – and another tramp with her.

CHRIS *starts for the entrance to the back room.*

MARTHY (*to* ANNA, *in a hurried, nervous whisper*). That's him
now. He's comin' in here. Brace up!

ANNA. Who?

CHRIS *opens the door.*

MARTHY (*as if she were greeting him for the first time*). Why hallo,
Old Chris. (*Then before he can speak, she shuffles hurriedly past him
into the bar, beckoning him to follow her.*) Come here. I wanta tell
yuh somethin'. (*He goes out to her. She speaks hurriedly in a low
voice.*) Listen! I'm goin' to beat it down to the barge – pack up
me duds and blow. That's her in there – your Anna – just
come – waitin' for yuh. Treat her right, see? She's been sick.

Well, s'long! (*She goes into the back room – to* ANNA.) S'long, kid.
I gotta beat it now. See yuh later.

ANNA (*nervously*). So long.

MARTHY *goes quickly out of the family entrance.*

LARRY (*looking at the stupefied* CHRIS *curiously*). Well, what's up
now?

CHRIS (*vaguely*). Nutting – nutting. (*He stands before the door to the
back room in an agony of embarrassed emotion – then he forces himself
to a bold decision, pushes open the door, and walks in. He stands there,
casts a shy glance at* ANNA, *whose brilliant clothes, and, to him, high-
toned appearance awe him terribly. He looks about him with pitiful
nervousness as if to avoid the appraising look with which she takes in
his face, his clothes, etc. – his voice seeming to plead for her
forbearance.*) Anna!

ANNA (*acutely embarrassed in her turn*). Hallo – father. She told me
it was you. I yust got here a little while ago.

CHRIS (*goes slowly over to her chair*). It's good – for see you– after
all dem years, Anna. (*He bends down over her. After an embarrassed
struggle they manage to kiss each other.*)

ANNA (*a trace of genuine feeling in her voice*). It's good to see you,
too.

CHRIS (*grasps her arms and looks into her face – then overcome by a
wave of fierce tenderness*). Anna lilla! Anna lilla! (*Takes her in his
arms.*)

ANNA (*shrinks away from him, half frightened*). What's that –
Swedish? I don't know it. (*Then as if seeking relief from the tension
in a voluble chatter.*) Gee, I had an awful trip coming here. I'm
all in. I had to sit up in the dirty coach all night – couldn't get
no sleep, hardly – and then I had a hard job finding this place.
I never been in New York before, you know, and –

CHRIS (*who has been staring down at her face admiringly, not hearing
what she says – impulsively*). You know you vas awful pooty gel,
Anna? Ay bet all men see you fall in love with you, py yiminy!

ANNA (*repelled – harshly*). Cut it! You talk same as they all do.

CHRIS (*hurt – humbly*). Ain't no harm for your fader talk dat vay,
Anna.

ANNA (*forcing a short laugh*). No – course not. Only – it's funny
to see you and not remember nothing. You're like – a stranger.

CHRIS (sadly). Ay s'pose. Ay never come home only few times ven you vas kit in Sveden. You don't remember dat?

ANNA. No (Resentfully.) But why didn't you never come home them days? Why didn't you never come out West to see me?

CHRIS (slowly). Ay tank, after your mo'der die, ven Ay vas avay on voyage, it's better for you don't never see me! (He sinks down in the chair opposite her dejectedly – then turns to her – sadly.) Ay don't know, Anna, vhy Ay never come home Sveden in ole year. Ay vant come home end of every voyage. Ay vant see your mo'der, your two bro'der before dey vas drowned, you ven you vas born – but – Ay – don't go. Ay sign on oder ships – go South America, go Australia, go China, go every port all over world many times – but Ay never go aboard ship sail for Sveden. Ven Ay gat money for pay passage home as passenger den – (He bows his head guiltily.) Ay forgat and Ay spend all money. Ven Ay tank again, it's too late. (He sighs.) Ay don't know vhy, but dat's vay with most sailor fallar, Anna. Dat ole davil sea make dem crazy fools with her dirty tricks. It's so.

ANNA (who has watched him keenly while he has been speaking – with a trace of scorn in her voice). Then you think the sea's to blame for everything, eh? Well, you're still workin' on it, ain't you, spite of all you used to write me about hating it. That dame was here told me you was captain of a coal barge – and you wrote me you was yanitor of a building!

CHRIS (embarrassed but lying glibly). Oh, Ay work on land long time as yanitor. Yust short time ago Ay got dis yob cause Ay was sick, need open air.

ANNA (sceptically). Sick? You? You'd never think it.

CHRIS. And, Anna, dis ain't real sailor yob. Dis ain't real boat on sea. She's yust ole tub – like piece of land with house on it dat float. Yob on her ain't sea yob. No. Ay don't gat yob on sea, Anna, if Ay die first. Ay swear dat, ven your mo'der die. Ay keep my word, py yingo!

ANNA (perplexed). Well, I can't see no difference. (Dismissing the subject.) Speaking of being sick, I been there myself – yust out of the hospital two weeks ago.

CHRIS (immediately all concern). You, Anna? Py golly! (Anxiously.) You feel better now, dough, don't you? You look little tired, dat's all!

ANNA (*wearily*). I am. Tired to death. I need a long rest and I don't see much chance of getting it.

CHRIS. What you mean, Anna?

ANNA. Well, when I made up my mind to come to see you, I thought you was a yanitor – that you'd have a place where, maybe, if you didn't mind having me, I could visit a while and rest up – till I felt able to get back on the job again.

CHRIS (*eagerly*). But Ay gat place, Anna – nice place. You rest all you want, py yiminy! You don't never have to vork as nurse gel no more. You stay with me, py golly!

ANNA (*surprised and pleased by his eagerness – with a smile*). Then you're really glad to see me – honest?

CHRIS (*pressing one of her hands in both of his*). Anna, Ay like see you like hell, Ay tal you! And don't you talk no more about gatting yob. You stay with me. Ay don't see you for long time, you don't forgat dat. (*His voice trembles.*) Ay'm gatting ole. Ay gat no one in vorld but you.

ANNA (*touched – embarrassed by this unfamiliar emotion*). Thanks. It sounds good to hear some one – talk to me that way. Say, though – if you're so lonely – it's funny – why ain't you ever married again?

CHRIS (*shaking his head emphatically – after a pause*). Ay love your mo'der too much for ever do dat, Anna.

ANNA (*impressed – slowly*). I don't remember nothing about her. What was she like? Tell me.

CHRIS. Ay tal you all about everytang – and you tal me all tangs happen to you. But not here now. Dis ain't good place for young gel, anyway. Only no good sailor fallar come here for gat drunk. (*He gets to his feet quickly and picks up her bag.*) You come with me, Anna. You need lie down, gat rest.

ANNA (*half-rises to her feet, then sits down again*). Where're you going?

CHRIS. Come. Ve gat on board.

ANNA (*disappointedly*). On board your barge, you mean? (*Dryly.*) Nix for mine! (*Then seeing his crestfallen look – forcing a smile.*) Do you think that's a good place for a young girl like me – a coal barge?

CHRIS (*dully*). Yes, Ay tank. (*He hesitates – then continues more and more pleadingly*.) You don't know how nice it's on barge, Anna. Tug come and ve gat towed out on voyage – yust water all round, and sun, and fresh air, and good grub for make you strong, healthy gel. You see many tangs you don't see before. You gat moonlight at night, maybe; see steamer pass; see schooner make sail – see everytang dat's pooty. You need take rest like dat. You work too hard for young gel already. You need vacation, yes!

ANNA (*who has listened to him with a growing interest – with an uncertain laugh*). It sounds good to hear you tell it. I'd sure like a trip on the water, all right. It's the barge idea has me stopped. Well, I'll go down with you and have a look – and maybe I'll take a chance. Gee, I'd do anything once.

CHRIS (*picks up her bag again*). Ve go, eh?

ANNA. What's the rush? Wait a second. (*Forgetting the situation for a moment, she relapses into the familar form and flashes one of her winning trade smiles at him*.) Gee, I'm thirsty.

CHRIS (*sets down her bag immediately – hastily*). Ay'm sorry, Anna. What you tank you like for drink, eh?

ANNA (*promptly*). I'll take a – (*Then suddenly reminded – confusedly*.) I don't know. What's they got here?

CHRIS (*with a grin*). Ay don't tank dey got much fancy drink for young gel in dis place, Anna. Yinger ale – sas' prilla, maybe.

ANNA (*forcing a laugh herself*). Make it sas, then.

CHRIS (*coming up to her – with a wink*). Ay tal you, Anna, ve calabrate, yes – dis one time because ve meet after many year. (*In a half-whisper, embarrassedly*.) Dey gat good port vine, Anna. It's good for you, Ay tank – little bit – for give you appetite. It ain't strong, neider. One glass don't go to your head, Ay promise.

ANNA (*with a half-hysterical laugh*). All right. I'll take port.

CHRIS. Ay go gat him. (*He goes out to the bar. As soon as the door closes*, ANNA *starts to her feet*.)

ANNA (*picking up her bag – half-aloud – stammeringly*). Gawd, I can't stand this! I better beat it. (*Then she lets her bag drop, stumbles over to her chair again, and covering her face with her hands, begins to sob*.)

LARRY (*putting down his paper as* CHRIS *comes up – with a grin*). Well, who's the blonde?

CHRIS (*proudly*). Dat vas Anna, Larry.

LARRY (*in amazement*). Your daughter, Anna?

CHRIS *nods.* LARRY *lets a long, low whistle escape him and turns away embarrassedly.*

CHRIS. Don't you tank she vas pooty gel, Larry?

LARRY (*rising to the occasion*). Sure! A peach!

CHRIS. You bet you! Give me drink for take back – one port vine for Anna – she calabrate dis one time with me – and small beer for me.

LARRY (*as he gets the drinks*). Small beer for you, eh? She's reformin' you already.

CHRIS (*pleased*). You bet! (*He takes the drinks. As she hears him coming,* ANNA *hastily dries her eyes, tries to smile.* CHRIS *comes in and sets the drinks down on the table – stares at her for a second anxiously – patting her hand.*) You look tired, Anna. Vell, Ay make you take good long rest now. (*Picking up his beer.*) Come, you drink vine. It put new life in you. (*She lifts her glass – he grins.*) Skoal, Anna! You know dat Swedish word?

ANNA. Skoal! (*Downing her port at a gulp like a drink of whisky – her lips trembling.*) Skoal! Guess I know that word, all right, all right!

The curtain falls.

ACT TWO

Ten days later. The stern of the deeply laden barge, Simeon Winthrop, *at anchor in the outer harbour of Provincetown, Mass. It is ten o'clock at night. Dense fog shrouds the barge on all sides, and she floats motionless on a calm. A lantern set up on an immense coil of thick hawser sheds a dull, filtering light on objects near it – the heavy steel bits for making fast the tow-lines, etc. In the rear is the cabin, its misty windows glowing wanly with the light of a lamp inside. The chimney of the cabin stove rises a few feet above the roof. The doleful tolling of bells, on Long Point, on ships at anchor, breaks the silence at regular intervals.*

As the curtain rises, ANNA *is discovered standing near the coil of rope on which the lantern is placed. She looks healthy, transformed, the natural colour has come back to her face. She has on a black, oilskin coat, but wears no hat. She is staring out into the fog astern with an expression of awed wonder. The cabin door is pushed open and* CHRIS *appears. He is dressed in yellow oilskins – coat, trousers, sou'wester – and wears high sea-boots.*

CHRIS (*the glare from the cabin still in his eyes, peers blinkingly astern*). Anna! (*Receiving no reply, he calls again, this time with apparent apprehension.*) Anna!

ANNA (*with a start – making a gesture with her hand as if to impose silence – in a hushed whisper*). Yes, here I am. What d'you want?

CHRIS (*walks over to her – solicitously*). Don't you come turn in, Anna? It's late – after four bells. It ain't good for you stay out here in fog, Ay tank.

ANNA. Why not? (*With a trace of strange exultation.*) I love this fog! Honest! It's so – (*She hesitates, groping for a word.*) – funny and still. I feel as if I was – out of things altogether.

CHRIS (*spitting disgustedly*). Fog's vorst one of her dirty tricks, py yingo!

ANNA (*with a short laugh*). Beefing about the sea again? I'm getting so's I love it, the little I've seen.

CHRIS (*glancing at her moodily*). Dat's foolish talk, Anna. You see her more, you don't talk dat vay. (*Then seeing her irritation, he hastily adopts a more cheerful tone.*) But Ay'm glad you like it on barge. Ay'm glad it makes you feel good again. (*With a placating grin.*) You like live like dis alone with ole fa'der eh?

ANNA. Sure I do. Everything's been so different from anything I ever come across before. And now – this fog – Gee, I wouldn't have missed it for nothing. I never thought living on ships was so different from land. Gee, I'd yust love to work on it, honest I would, if I was a man. I don't wonder you always been a sailor.

CHRIS (*vehemently*). Ay ain't sailor, Anna. And dis ain't real sea. You only see nice part. (*Then as she doesn't answer, he continues hopefully.*) Vell, fog lift in morning, Ay tank.

ANNA (*the exultation again in her voice*). I love it! I don't give a rap if it never lifts! (CHRIS *fidgets from one foot to the other worriedly.* ANNA *continues slowly, after a pause.*) It makes me feel clean – out here – 's if I'd taken a bath.

CHRIS (*after a pause*). You better go in cabin – read book. Dat put you to sleep.

ANNA. I don't want to sleep. I want to stay out here – and think about things.

CHRIS (*walks away from her toward the cabin – then comes back*). You act funny tonight, Anna.

ANNA (*her voice rising angrily*). Say, what're you trying to do – make things rotten? You been kind as kind can be to me and I certainly appreciate it – only don't spoil it all now. (*Then, seeing the hurt expression on her father's face, she forces a smile.*) Let's talk of something else. Come. Sit down here. (*She points to the coil of rope.*)

CHRIS (*sits down beside her with a sigh*). It's gatting pooty late in night, Anna. Must be near five bells.

ANNA (*interestedly*). Five bells? What time is that?

CHRIS. Half past ten.

ANNA. Funny I don't know nothing about sea talk – but those cousins was always talking crops and that stuff. Gee, wasn't I sick of it – and of them!

CHRIS. You don't like live on farm, Anna?

ANNA. I've told you a hundred times I hated it (*Decidedly.*) I'd rather have one drop of ocean than all the farms in the world! Honest! And you wouldn't like a farm, neither. Here's where you belong. (*She makes a sweeping gesture seaward.*) But not on a coal barge. You belong on a real ship, sailing all over the world.

CHRIS (*moodily*). Ay've done dat many year, Anna, when Ay vas damn fool.

ANNA (*disgustedly*). Oh, rats! (*After a pause she speaks musingly.*) Was the men in our family always sailors – as far back as you know about?

CHRIS (*shortly*). Yes. Damn fools! All men in our village on coast, Sveden, go to sea. Ain't nutting else for dem to do. My fa'der die on board ship in Indian Ocean. He's buried at sea. Ay don't never know him only little bit. Den my tree bro'der, older'n me, dey go on ships. Den Ay go, too. Den my mo'der she's left all 'lone. She die pooty quick after dat – all 'lone. Ve vas all avay on voyage when she die. (*He pauses sadly.*) Two my bro'der dey gat lost on fishing boat same like your bro'ders vas drowned. My oder bro'der, he save money, give up sea, den he die home in bed. He's only one dat ole davil don't kill. (*Defiantly.*) But me, Ay bet you Ay die ashore in bed, too!

ANNA. Were all of 'em yust plain sailors?

CHRIS. Able body seaman, most of dem. (*With a certain pride.*) Dey vas all smart seaman, too – A1. (*Then after hesitating a moment – shyly.*) Ay was bos'n.

ANNA. Bos'n?

CHRIS. Dat's kind of officer.

ANNA. Gee, that was fine. What does he do?

CHRIS (*after a second's hesitation, plunged into gloom again by his fear of her enthusiasm*). Hard vork all time. It's rotten. Ay tal you, for go to sea. (*Determined to disgust her with sea life – volubly.*) Dey're all fool fallar, dem fallar in our family. Dey all vork rotten yob on sea for nutting, don't care nutting but yust gat big pay-day in pocket, gat drunk, gat robbed, ship avay again on oder voyage. Dey don't come home. Dey don't do anytang like good man do. And dat ole davil, sea, sooner, later she svallow dem up.

ANNA (*with an excited laugh*). Good sports, I'd call 'em. (*Then hastily.*) But say – listen – did all the women of the family marry sailors?

CHRIS (*eagerly – seeing a chance to drive home his point*). Yes – and it's bad on dem like hell vorst of all. Dey don't see deir men only once in long while. Dey set and vait all 'lone. And vhen deir boys grow up, go to sea, dey sit and vait some more. (*Vehemently.*) Any gel marry sailor, she's crazy fool! Your mo'der she tal you same tang if she vas alive. (*He relapses into an attitude of sombre brooding.*)

ANNA (*after a pause – dreamily*). Funny! I do feel sort of – nutty, tonight. I feel old.

CHRIS (*mystified*). Ole?

ANNA. Sure – like I'd been living a long, long time – out here in the fog. (*Frowning perplexedly.*) I don't know how to tell you yust what I mean. It's like I'd come home after a long visit away some place. It all seems like I'd been here before lots of times – on boats – in this same fog. (*With a short laugh.*) You must think I'm off my base.

CHRIS (*gruffly*). Anybody feel funny dat vay in fog.

ANNA (*persistently*). But why d'you s'pose I feel so – like I'd found something I'd missed and been looking for – 's if this was the right place for me to fit in? And I seem to have forgot – everything that's happened – like it didn't matter no more. And I feel clean, somehow – like you feel yust after you've took a bath. And I feel happy for once – yes, honest! – happier than I ever been anywhere before! (*As* CHRIS *makes no comment but a heavy sigh, she continues wonderingly.*) It's nutty for me to feel that way, don't you think?

CHRIS (*a grim foreboding in his voice*). Ay tank Ay'm damn fool for bring you on voyage, Anna.

ANNA (*impressed by his tone*). You talk – nutty tonight yourself. You act's if you was scared something was going to happen.

CHRIS. Only God know dat, Anna.

ANNA (*half-mockingly*). Then it'll be Gawd's will, like the preachers say – what does happen.

CHRIS (*starts to his feet with fierce protest*). No! Dat ole davil, sea, she ain't God! (*In the pause of silence that comes after his defiance a hail in a man's husky, exhausted voice comes faintly out of the fog to port. 'Ahoy!' CHRIS gives a startled exclamation.*)

ANNA (*jumping to her feet*). What's that?

CHRIS (*who has regained his composure – sheepishly*). Py golly, dat scare me for minute. It's only some fallar hail, Anna – loose his course in fog. Must be fisherman's power boat. His engine break down, Ay guess. (*The 'Ahoy' comes again through the wall of fog, sounding much nearer this time. CHRIS goes over to the port bulwark.*)

Sound from dis side. She come in from open sea. (*He holds his hands to his mouth, megaphone-fashion, and shouts back.*) Ahoy dere! Vhat's trouble?

THE VOICE (*this time sounding nearer but up forward toward the bow*). Heave a rope when we come alongside. (*Then irritably.*) Where are ye, ye scut?

CHRIS. Ay hear dem rowing. Dey come up by bow, Ay tank. (*Then shouting out again.*) Dis vay!

THE VOICE. Right ye are! (*There is a muffled sound of oars in rowlocks.*)

ANNA (*half to herself – resentfully*). Why don't that guy stay where he belongs?

CHRIS (*hurriedly*). Ay go up bow. All hands asleep 'cepting fallar on vatch. Ay gat heave line to dat fallar. (*He picks up a coil of rope and hurries off toward the bow.*)

ANNA *walks back toward the extreme stern as if she wanted to remain as much isolated as possible. She turns her back on the proceedings and stares out into the fog.* THE VOICE *is heard again shouting* 'Ahoy' *and* CHRIS *answering* 'Dis vay.' *Then there is a pause – the murmur of excited voices – then the scuffling of feet.* CHRIS *appears from around the cabin to port. He is supporting the limp form of a man dressed in dungarees, holding one of the man's arms around his neck. The deckhand,* JOHNSON, *a young, blond Swede, follows him, helping along another exhausted man similar fashion.* ANNA *turns to look at them.* CHRIS *stops for a second.*

CHRIS (*volubly*). Anna! You come help, vill you? You find vhisky in cabin. Dese fallars need drink for fix dem. Dey vas near dead.

ANNA (*hurrying to him*). Sure – but who are they? What's the trouble?

CHRIS. Sailor fallars. Deir steamer gat wrecked. Dey been five days in open boat – four fallars – only one left able stand up. Come, Anna. (*She precedes him into the cabin, holding the door open while he and* JOHNSON *carry in their burdens. The door is shut, then opened again as* JOHNSON *comes out.* CHRIS's *voice shouts after him.*) Go gat oder fallar, Yohnson.

JOHNSON. Yes, sir.

He goes. The door is closed again. MAT BURKE *stumbles in around the port side of the cabin. He moves slowly, feeling his way uncertainly, keeping hold of the port bulwark with his right hand to steady himself.*

He is stripped to the waist, has on nothing but a pair of dirty dungaree trousers. He is a powerful, broad-chested six footer, his face handsome in a hard, rough, bold, defiant way. He is about thirty, in the full power of his heavy-muscled, immense strength. His dark eyes are bloodshot and wild from sleeplessness. The muscles of his arms and shoulders are lumped in knots and bunches, the veins of his forearms stand out like blue cords. He finds his way to the coil of hawser and sits down on it facing the cabin, his back bowed, head in his hands in an attitude of spent weariness.

BURKE *(talking aloud to himself)*. Row, ye divil! Row! *(Then lifting his head and looking about him.)* What's this tub? Well, we're safe, anyway – with the help of God. *(He makes the sign of the cross mechanically. JOHNSON comes along the deck to port, supporting the fourth man, who is babbling to himself incoherently. BURKE glances at him disdainfully.)* Is it losing the small wits ye iver had, ye are? Deck-scrubbing scut! *(They pass him and go into the cabin, leaving the door open. BURKE sags forward wearily.)* I'm bate out – bate out entirely.

ANNA comes out of the cabin with a tumbler quarter-full of whisky in her hand. She gives a start when she sees BURKE so near her, the light from the open door falling full on him. Then, overcoming what is evidently a feeling of repulsion, she comes up beside him.

ANNA. Here you are. Here's a drink for you. You need it, I guess.

BURKE *(lifting his head slowly – confusedly)*. Is it dreaming I am?

ANNA *(half-smiling)*. Drink it and you'll find it ain't no dream.

BURKE. To hell with the drink – but I'll take it just the same. *(He tosses it down.)* Aah! I'm needin' that – and 'tis fine stuff. *(Looking up at her with frank, grinning admiration.)* But 'twasn't the booze I meant when I said, was I dreaming. I thought you was some mermaid out of the sea come to torment me. *(He reaches out to feel her arm.)* Aye, rale flesh and blood, divil a less.

ANNA *(coldly. Stepping back from him)*. Cut that.

BURKE. But tell me, isn't this a barge I'm on – or isn't it?

ANNA. Sure.

BURKE. And what is a fine, handsome woman the like of you doing on this scow?

ANNA *(coldly)*. Never you mind. *(Then half-amused in spite of herself.)* Say, you're a great one, honest – starting right in kidding after what you been through.

BURKE (*delighted – proudly*). Ah, it was nothing – aisy for a rale man with guts to him, the like of me. (*He laughs.*) All in the day's work, darlin'. (*Then, more seriously, but still in a boastful tone, confidentially.*) But I won't be denying 'twas a damn narrow squeak. We'd all ought to be with Davy Jones at the bottom of the sea, be rights. And only for me, I'm telling you, and the great strength and guts is in me, we'd be being scoffed by the fishes this minute!

ANNA (*contemptuously*). Gee, you hate yourself, don't you? (*Then turning away from him indifferently.*) Well, you'd better come in and lie down. You must want to sleep.

BURKE (*stung – rising unsteadily to his feet with chest out and head thrown back – resentfully*). Lie down and sleep, is it? Divil a wink I'm after having for two days and nights and divil a bit I'm needing now. Let you not be thinking I'm the like of them three weak scuts come in the boat with me. I could lick the three of them sitting down with one hand tied behind me. They may be bate out, but I'm not – and I've been rowing the boat with them lying in the bottom not able to raise a hand for the last two days we was in it. (*Furiously, as he sees this is making no impression on her.*) And I can lick all hands on this tub, wan be wan, tired as I am!

ANNA (*sarcastically*). Gee, ain't you a hard guy! (*Then, with a trace of sympathy, as she notices him swaying from weakness.*) But never mind that fight talk. I'll take your word for all you've said. Go on and sit down out here, anyway, if I can't get you to come inside. (*He sits down weakly.*) You're all in, you might as well own up to it.

BURKE (*fiercely*). The hell I am!

ANNA (*coldly*). Well, be stubborn then for all I care. And I must say I don't care for your language. The men I know don't pull that rough stuff when ladies are around.

BURKE (*getting unsteadily to his feet again – in a rage*). Ladies! Ho-ho! Divil mend you! Let you not be making game of me. What would ladies be doing on this bloody hulk? (*As ANNA attempts to go to the cabin, he lurches into her path.*) Aisy, now! You're not the old Square-head's woman, I suppose you'll be telling me next – living in his cabin with him, no less! (*Seeing the cold, hostile expression on ANNA's face, he suddenly changes his tone to one of boisterous joviality.*) But I do be thinking, iver since the first look my eyes took at you, that it's a fool you are to be wasting yourself – a fine, handsome girl – on a stumpy runt of a man like that old Swede. There's too many strapping great lads on the sea would give their heart's blood for one kiss of you!

ANNA (*scornfully*). Lads like you, eh?

BURKE (*grinning*). Ye take the words out o' my mouth. I'm the proper lad for you, if it's meself do be saying it. (*With a quick movement he puts his arms about her waist.*) Whisht, now, me daisy! Himself's in the cabin. It's wan of your kisses I'm needing to take the tiredness from me bones. Wan kiss, now! (*He presses her to him and attempts to kiss her.*)

ANNA (*struggling fiercely*). Leggo of me, you big mut!

She pushes him away with all her might. BURKE, weak and tottering, is caught off his guard. He is thrown down backward, and, in falling, hits his head a hard thump against the bulwark. He lies there still, knocked out for the moment. ANNA stands for a second, looking down at him anxiously. Then she kneels down beside him and raises his head to her knee, staring into his face for some sign of life.

BURKE (*stirring a bit – mutteringly*). God stiffen it! (*He opens his eyes and blinks up at her with vague wonder.*)

ANNA (*letting his head sink back on the deck, rising to her feet with a sigh of relief*). You're coming to all right, eh? Gee, I was scared for a moment I'd killed you.

BURKE (*with difficulty rising to a sitting position – scornfully*). Killed, is it? It'd take more than a bit of a blow to crack my thick skull. (*Then looking at her with the most intense admiration.*) But, glory be, it's a power of strength is in them two fine arms of yours. There's not a man in the world can say the same as you, that he seen Mat Burke lying at his feet and him dead to the world.

ANNA (*rather remorsefully*). Forget it. I'm sorry it happened, see? (*BURKE rises and sits on bench. Then severely.*) Only you had no right to be getting fresh with me. Listen, now, and don't go getting any more wrong notions. I'm on this barge because I'm making a trip with my father. The captain's my father. Now you know.

BURKE. The old square – the old Swede, I mean?

ANNA. Yes.

BURKE (*rising – peering at her face*). Sure, I might have known it, if I wasn't a bloody fool from birth. Where else'd you get that fine yellow hair is like a golden crown on your head.

ANNA (*with an amused laugh*). Say, nothing stops you, does it? (*Then attempting a severe tone again.*) But don't you think you ought to be apologizing for what you said and done yust a minute ago, instead of trying to kid me with that mush?

BURKE (*indignantly*). Mush! (*Then bending forward toward her with very intense earnestness.*) Indade, and I will ask your pardon a thousand times – and on my knees, if ye like. I didn't mean a word of what I said or did. (*Resentful again for a second.*) But divil a woman in all the ports of the world has iver made a great fool of me that way before!

ANNA (*with amused sarcasm*). I see. You mean you're a lady-killer and they all fall for you.

BURKE (*offended. Passionately*). Leave off your fooling! 'Tis that is after getting my back up at you. (*Earnestly.*) 'Tis no lie I'm telling you about the women. (*Ruefully.*) Though it's a great jackass I am to be mistaking you, even in anger, for the like of them cows on the water-front is the only women I've met up with since I was growed to a man. (*As ANNA shrinks away from him at this, he hurries on pleadingly.*) I'm a hard, rough man, and I'm not fit, I'm thinking, to be kissing the shoe-soles of a fine, dacent girl the like of yourself. 'Tis only the ignorance of your kind made me see you wrong. So you'll forgive me, for the love of God, and let us be friends from this out. (*Passionately.*) I'm thinking I'd rather be friends with you than have my wish for anything else in the world. (*He holds out his hand to her shyly.*)

ANNA (*looking queerly at him, perplexed and worried, but moved and pleased in spite of herself – takes his hand uncertainly*). Sure.

BURKE (*with boyish delight*). God bless you! (*In his excitement he squeezes her hand tight.*)

ANNA. Ouch!

BURKE (*hastily dropping her hand – ruefully*). Your pardon, Miss. 'Tis a clumsy ape I am. (*Then simply – glancing down his arm proudly.*) It's great power I have in my hand and arm, and I do be forgetting it at times.

ANNA (*nursing her crushed hand and glancing at his arm, not without a trace of his own admiration*). Gee, you're some strong, all right.

BURKE (*delighted*). It's no lie, and why shouldn't I be, with me shovelling a million tons of coal in the stokeholes of ships since I was a lad only. (*He pats the coil of hawser invitingly.*) Let you sit down, now, Miss, and I'll be telling you a bit of myself, and you'll be telling me a bit of yourself, and in an hour we'll be as old friends as if we was born in the same house. (*He pulls at her sleeve shyly.*) Sit down now, if you plaze.

ANNA (*with a half-laugh*). Well – (*She sits down.*) But we won't talk about me, see? You tell me about yourself and about the wreck.

BURKE (*flattered*). I'll tell you, surely. But can I be asking you one question, Miss, has my head in a puzzle?

ANNA (*guardedly*). Well – I dunno – what is it?

BURKE. What is it you do when you're not taking a trip with the Old Man? For I'm thinking a fine girl the like of you ain't living always on this tub.

ANNA (*uneasily*). No – of course I ain't (*She searches his face suspiciously, afraid there may be some hidden insinuation in his words. Seeing his simple frankness, she goes on confidently.*) Well, I'll tell you. I'm a governess, see? I take care of kids for people and learn them things.

BURKE (*impressed*). A governess, is it? You must be smart, surely.

ANNA. But let's not talk about me. Tell me about the wreck, like you promised me you would.

BURKE (*importantly*). 'Twas this way, Miss. Two weeks out we ran into the divil's own storm, and she sprang wan hell of a leak up for 'ard. The skipper was hoping to make Boston before another blow would finish her, but ten days back we met up with another storm the like of the first, only worse. Four days we was in it with green seas raking over her from bow to stern. That was a terrible time, God help us. (*Proudly.*) And if 'twasn't for me and my great strength, I'm telling you – and it's God's truth – there'd been mutiny itself in the stokehole. 'Twas me held them to it, with a kick to wan and a clout to another, and they not caring a damn for the engineers any more, but fearing a clout of my right arm more than they'd fear the sea itself. (*He glances at her anxiously, eager for her approval.*)

ANNA (*concealing a smile – amused by this boyish boasting of his*). You did some hard work, didn't you?

BURKE (*promptly*). I did that! I'm a divil for sticking it out when them that's weak give up. But much good it did anyone! 'Twas a mad, fightin' scramble in the last seconds with each man for himself. I disremember how it come about, but there was the four of us in wan boat, and when we was raised high on a great

wave I took a look about and divil a sight there was of ship or
men on top of the sea.

ANNA (*in a subdued voice*). Then all the others was drowned?

BURKE. They was, surely.

ANNA (*with a shudder*). What a terrible end!

BURKE (*turns to her*). A terrible end for the like of them swabs
does live on land, maybe. But for the like of us does be
roaming the seas, a good end, I'm telling you – quick and clane.

ANNA (*struck by the word*). Yes, clean. That's yust the word for –
all of it – the way it makes me feel.

BURKE. The sea, you mean? (*Interestedly.*) I'm thinking you have
a bit of it in your blood, too. Your Old Man wasn't only a barge
rat – begging your pardon – all his life, by the cut of him.

ANNA. No, he was bo'sun on sailing ships for years. And all the
men on both sides of the family have gone to sea as far back as
he remembers, he says. All the women have married sailors, too.

BURKE (*with intense satisfaction*). Did they, now? They had spirit
in them. It's only on the sea you'd find rale men with guts is fit
to wed with fine, high-tempered girls – (*Then he adds half-boldly.*)
– the like of yourself.

ANNA (*with a laugh*). There you go kiddin' again. (*Then seeing his
hurt expression – quickly.*) But you was going to tell me about
yoursef. You're Irish, of course I can tell that.

BURKE (*stoutly*). Yes, thank God, though I've not seen a sight of
it in fifteen years or more.

ANNA (*thoughtfully*). Sailors never do go home hardly, do they?
That's what my father was saying.

BURKE. He wasn't telling no lie. (*With sudden melancholy.*) It's a
hard and lonesome life, the sea is. The only women you'd meet
in the ports of the world who'd be willing to speak you a kind
word isn't women at all. You know the kind I mane, and
they're a poor, wicked lot, God forgive them. They're looking
to steal the money from you only.

ANNA (*her face averted – rising to her feet – agitatedly*). I think – I
guess I'd better see what's doing inside.

BURKE (*afraid he has offended her – beseechingly*). Don't go, I'm
saying! Is it I've given you offence with my talk of the like of
them? Don't heed it at all! I'm clumsy in my wits when it comes

to talking proper with a girl the like of you. And why wouldn't I be? Since the day I left home for me to go to sea punching coal, this is the first time I've had a word with a rale, dacent woman. So don't turn your back on me now, and we beginning to be friends.

ANNA (*turning to him again – forcing a smile*). I'm not sore at you, honest.

BURKE (*gratefully*). God bless you!

ANNA (*changing the subject abruptly*). But if you honestly think the sea's such a rotten life, why don't you get out of it?

BURKE (*surprised*). Work on land, is it? (*She nods. He spits scornfully.*) Digging spuds in the muck from dawn to dark, I suppose? (*Vehemently.*) I wasn't made for it, Miss.

ANNA (*with a laugh*). I thought you'd say that.

BURKE (*argumentatively*). But there's good jobs and bad jobs at sea, like there'd be on land. I'm thinking if it's in the stokehole of a proper liner I was, I'd be able to have a little house and be home to it wan week out of four. And I'm thinking that maybe then I'd have the luck to find a fine dacent girl – the like of yourself, now – would be willing to wed with me.

ANNA (*turning away from him with a short laugh – uneasily.*) Why, sure. Why not?

BURKE (*edging up close to her – exultantly*). Then you think a girl the like of yourself might maybe not mind the past at all but only be seeing the good herself put in me?

ANNA (*in the same tone*). Why, sure.

BURKE (*passionately*). She'd not be sorry for it, I'd take my oath! 'Tis no more drinking and roving about I'd be doing then, but giving my pay-day into her hand and staying at home with her as meek as a lamb each night of the week I'd be in port.

ANNA (*moved in spite of herself and troubled by this half-concealed proposal – with a forced laugh*). All you got to do is find the girl.

BURKE. I have found her!

ANNA (*half-frightened – trying to laugh it off*). You have? When? I thought you was saying –

BURKE (*boldly and forcefully*). This night. (*Hanging his head – humbly.*) If she'll be having me. (*Then raising his eyes to hers – simply.*) 'Tis you I mean.

ANNA (*is held by his eyes for a moment – then shrinks back from him with a strange, broken laugh*). Say – are you – going crazy? Are you trying to kid me? Proposing – to me – for Gawd's sake! – on such short acquaintance?

CHRIS *comes out of the cabin and stands staring blinkingly astern. When he makes out ANNA in such intimate proximity to this strange sailor, an angry expression comes over his face.*

BURKE (*following her – with fierce, pleading insistence*). I'm telling you there's the will of God in it that brought me safe through the storm and fog to the wan spot in the world where you was! Think of that now, and isn't it queer –

CHRIS. Anna! (*He comes toward them, raging, his fists clenched.*) Anna, you gat in cabin, you hear!

ANNA (*all her emotions immediately transformed into resentment at his bullying tone*). Who d'you think you're talking to – a slave?

CHRIS (*hurt – his voice breaking – pleadingly*). You need gat rest, Anna. You gat sleep. (*She does not move. He turns on BURKE furiously.*) What you doing here, you sailor fallar? You ain't sick like oders. You gat in fo'c'sle. Dey give you bunk. (*Threateningly.*) You hurry. Ay tal you!

ANNA (*impulsively*). But he is sick. Look at him. He can hardly stand up.

BURKE (*straightening and throwing out his chest – with a bold laugh*). Is it giving me orders ye are, me bucko? Let you look out then! With wan hand, weak as I am, I can break ye in two and fling the pieces over the side – and your crew after you. (*Stopping abruptly.*) I was forgetting. You're her Old Man, and I'd not raise a fist to you for the world.

His knees sag, he wavers and seems about to fall. ANNA utters an exclamation of alarm and hurries to his side.

ANNA (*taking one of his arms over her shoulder*). Come on in the cabin. You can have my bed if there ain't no other place.

BURKE (*with jubilant happiness – as they proceed toward the cabin*). Glory be to God, is it holding my arm about your neck you are! Anna! Anna! Sure, it's a sweet name is suited to you.

ANNA (*guiding him carefully*). Sssh! Sssh!

BURKE. Whisht, is it? Indade, and I'll not. I'll be roaring it out like a fog horn over the sea! You're the girl of the world, and we'll be marrying soon, and I don't care who knows it!

ANNA (*as she guides him through the cabin door*). Ssshh! Never mind that talk. You go to sleep.

They go out of sight in the cabin. CHRIS, *who has been listening to* BURKE's *last words with open-mouthed amazement, stands looking after them helplessly.*

CHRIS (*turns suddenly and shakes his fist out at the sea – with bitter hatred*). Dat's your dirty trick, damn ole davil, you! (*Then in a frenzy of rage.*) But, py God, you don't do dat! Not while Ay'm living! No, py God, you don't!

The curtain falls.

ACT THREE

The interior of the cabin on the barge, Simeon Winthrop *(at dock in Boston) – a narrow, low-ceilinged compartment, the walls of which are painted a light brown with white trimmings. In the rear on the left, a door leading to the sleeping quarters. In the far left corner, a large locker-closet, painted white, on the door of which a mirror hangs on a nail. In the rear wall, two small square windows and a door opening out on the deck toward the stern. In the right wall, two more windows looking out on the port deck. White curtains, clean and stiff, are at the windows. A table with two cane-bottomed chairs stands in the centre of the cabin. A dilapidated, wicker rocker, painted brown, is also by the table.*

It is afternoon of a sunny day about a week later. From the harbour and docks outside, muffled by the closed door and windows, comes the sound of steamers' whistles and the puffing snort of the donkey engines of some ship unloading near by.

As the curtain rises, CHRIS *and* ANNA *are discovered.* ANNA *is seated in the rocking-chair by the table, with a newspaper in her hands. She is not reading but staring straight in front of her. She looks unhappy, troubled, frowningly concentrated on her thoughts.* CHRIS *wanders about the room, casting quick, uneasy side glances at her face, then stopping to peer absent-mindedly out of the window. His attitude betrays an overwhelming, gloomy anxiety which has him on tenterhooks. He pretends to be engaged in setting things shipshape, but this occupation is confined to picking up some object, staring at it stupidly for a second, then aimlessly putting it down again. He clears his throat and starts to sing to himself in a low, doleful voice:* 'My Yosephine, come aboard de ship. Long time Ay vait for you.'

ANNA (*turning on him, sarcastically*). I'm glad someone's feeling good (*Wearily.*) Gee, I sure wish we was out of this dump and back in New York.

CHRIS (*with a sigh*). Ay'm glad when ve sail again, too. (*Then, as she makes no comment, he goes on with a ponderous attempt at sarcasm.*) Ay don't see vhy you don't like Boston, dough. You have good time here, Ay tank. You go ashore all time, every day and night veek ve've been here. You go to movies, see show, gat all kinds fun – (*His eyes hard with hatred.*) All with that damn Irish fallar!

ANNA (*with weary scorn*). Oh, for heaven's sake, are you off on that again? Where's the harm in his taking me around? D'you want me to sit all day and night in this cabin with you – and knit? Ain't I got a right to have as good a time as I can?

CHRIS. It ain't right kind of fun – not with that fallar, no.

ANNA. I been back on board every night by eleven, ain't I?

(*Then struck by some thought – looks at him with keen suspicion – with rising anger.*) Say, look here, what d'you mean by what you yust said?

CHRIS (*hastily*). Nutting but what Ay say, Anna.

ANNA. You said 'ain't right' and you said it funny. Say, listen here, you ain't trying to insinuate that there's something wrong between us, are you?

CHRIS (*horrified*). No, Anna! No, Ay svear to God, Ay never tank dat!

ANNA (*mollified by his very evident sincerity – sitting down again*). Well, don't you never think it neither if you want me ever to speak to you again. (*Angrily again.*) If I ever dreamt you thought that, I'd get the hell out of this barge so quick you couldn't see me for dust.

CHRIS (*soothingly*). Ay wouldn't never dream – (*Then, after a second's pause, reprovingly.*) You vas gatting learn to svear. Dat ain't nice for young gel, you tank?

ANNA (*with a faint trace of a smile*). Excuse me. You ain't used to such language, I know. (*Mockingly.*) That's what your taking me to sea has done for me.

CHRIS (*indignantly*). No, it ain't me. It's dat damn sailor fallar learn you bad tangs.

ANNA. He ain't a sailor. He's a stoker.

CHRIS (*forcibly*). Dat vas million times vorse, Ay tal you! Dem fallars dat vork below shovelling coal vas de dirtiest, rough gang of no-good fallars in vorld!

ANNA. I'd hate to hear you say that to Mat.

CHRIS. Oh, Ay tal him same tang. You don't gat it in head Ay'm scared of him yust 'cause he vas stronger'n Ay vas. (*Menacingly.*) You don't gat for fight with fists with dem fallars. Dere's oder vay for fix him.

ANNA (*glancing at him with sudden alarm*). What d'you mean?

CHRIS (*sullenly*). Nutting.

ANNA. You'd better not. I wouldn't start no trouble with him if I was you. He might forget some time that you was old and my father – and then you'd be out of luck.

CHRIS (*with smouldering hatred*). Vell, yust let him! Ay'm ole bird maybe, but Ay bet Ay show him trick or two.

ANNA (*suddenly changing her tone – persuasively*). Aw come on, be good. What's eating you, anyway? Don't you want no one to be nice to me except yourself?

CHRIS (*placated – coming to her – eagerly*). Yes, Ay do, Anna – only not fallar on sea. But Ay like for you marry steady fallar got good yob on land. You have little home in country all your own –

ANNA (*rising to her feet – brusquely*). Oh, cut it out! (*Scornfully.*) Little home in the country! I wish you could have seen the little home in the country where you had me in jail till I was sixteen! (*With rising irritation.*) Some day you're going to get me so mad with that talk, I'm going to turn loose on you and tell you – a lot of things that'll open your eyes.

CHRIS (*alarmed*). Ay don't vant –

ANNA. I know you don't; but you keep on talking yust the same.

CHRIS. Ay don't talk no more den, Anna.

ANNA. Then promise me you'll cut out saying nasty things about Mat Burke every chance you get.

CHRIS (*evasive and suspicious*). Vhy? You like dat fallar – very much, Anna?

ANNA. Yes, I certainly do! He's a regular man, no matter what faults he's got. One of his fingers is worth all the hundreds of men I met out there – inland.

CHRIS (*his face darkening*). Maybe you tank you love him, den?

ANNA (*defiantly*). What of it if I do.

CHRIS (*scowling and forcing out the words*). Maybe – you tank you – marry him?

ANNA (shaking her head). No! (CHRIS's *face lights up with relief.* ANNA *continues slowly, a trace of sadness in her voice.*) If I'd met him four years ago – or even two years ago – I'd have jumped at the chance, I tell you that straight. And I would now – only he's such a simple guy – a big kid – and I ain't got the heart to fool him. (*She breaks off suddenly.*) But don't never say again he ain't good enough for me. It's me ain't good enough for him.

CHRIS (*snorts scornfully*). Py yiminy, you go crazy, Ay tank!

ANNA (*with a mournful laugh*). Well, I been thinking I was myself the last few days. (*She goes and takes a shawl from a hook near the door and throws it over her shoulders*). Guess I'll take a walk down to the end of the dock for a minute and see what's doing. I love to watch the ships passing. Mat'll be along before long, I guess. Tell him where I am, will you?

CHRIS (*despondently*). All right, Ay tal him.

ANNA *goes out the doorway on rear.* CHRIS *follows her out and stands on the deck outside for a moment looking after her. Then he comes back inside and shuts the door. He stands looking out of the window – mutters – 'Dirty ole davil, you.' Then he goes to the table, sets the cloth straight mechanically, picks up the newspaper* ANNA *has let fall to the floor, and sits down in the rocking-chair. He stares at the paper for a while, then puts it on the table, holds his head in his hands, and sighs drearily. The noise of a man's heavy footsteps comes from the deck outside and there is a loud knock on the door.* CHRIS *starts, makes a move as if to get up and go to the door, then thinks better of it and sits still. The knock is repeated – then as no answer comes, the door is flung open and* MAT BURKE *appears.* CHRIS *scowls at the intruder and his hand instinctively goes back to the sheath knife on his hip.* BURKE *is dressed up – wears a cheap blue suit, a striped cotton shirt with a black tie, and black shoes newly shined. His face is beaming with good humour.*

BURKE (*as he sees* CHRIS – *in a jovial tone of mockery*). Well, God bless who's here! (*He bends down and squeezes his huge form through the narrow doorway.*) And how is the world treating you this afternoon, Anna's father?

CHRIS (*sullenly*). Pooty goot – if it ain't for some fallars.

BURKE (*with a grin*). Meaning me, do you? (*He laughs.*) Well, if you ain't the funny old crank of a man! (*Then soberly.*) Where's herself? (CHRIS *sits dumb, scowling, his eyes averted.* BURKE *is irritated by this silence.*) Where's Anna, I'm after asking you?

CHRIS (*hesitating – then grouchily*). She go down end of dock.

BURKE. I'll be going down to her, then. But first I'm thinking I'll take this chance when we're alone to have a word with you. (*He sits down opposite* CHRIS *at the table and leans over toward him.*) And that word is soon said. I'm marrying your Anna before this day is out, and you might as well make up your mind to it whether you like it or no.

CHRIS (*glaring at him with hatred and forcing a scornful laugh*). Hoho! Dat's easy for say!

BURKE. You mean I won't (*Scornfully.*) Is it the like of yourself will stop me, are you thinking?

CHRIS. Yes, Ay stop it, if it come to vorst.

BURKE (*with scornful pity*). God help you!

CHRIS. But ain't no need for me do dat. Anna –

BURKE (*smiling confidently*). Is it Anna you think will prevent me?

CHRIS. Yes.

BURKE. And I'm telling you she'll not. She knows I'm loving her, and she loves me the same, and I know it.

CHRIS. Ho-ho! She only have fun. She make big fool of you, dat's all!

BURKE (*unshaken – pleasantly*). That's a lie in your throat, divil mend you!

CHRIS. No, it ain't lie. She tal me yust before she go out she never marry fallar like you.

BURKE. I'll not believe it. 'Tis a great old liar you are, and a divil to be making a power of trouble if you had your way. But 'tis not trouble I'm looking for, and me sitting down here. (*Earnestly.*) Let us be talking it out now as man to man. You're her father, and wouldn't it be a shame for us to be at each other's throats like a pair of dogs, and I married with Anna. So out with the truth, man alive. What is it you're holding against me at all?

CHRIS (*a bit placated, in spite of himself, by* BURKE's *evident sincerity – but puzzled and suspicious.*) Vell – Ay don't vant for Anna gat married. Listen, you fallar. Ay'm a ole man. Ay don't see Anna for fifteen year. She vas all Ay gat in vorld. And now ven she come on first trip – you tank Ay vant her leave me 'lone again?

BURKE (*heartily*). Let you not be thinking I have no heart at all for the way you'd be feeling.

CHRIS (*astonished and encouraged – trying to plead persuasively*). Den you do right tang, eh? You ship avay again, leave Anna alone. (*Cajolingly.*) Big fallar like you dat's on sea, he don't need vife. He gat new gel in every port, you know dat.

BURKE (*angry for a second*). God stiffen you! (*Then controlling himself – calmly.*) I'll not be giving you the lie on that. But divil take you, there's a time comes to every man, on sea or land, that isn't a born fool, when he's sick of the lot of them cows, and wearing his heart out to meet up with a fine dacent girl, and have a home to call his own and be rearing up children in it. 'Tis small use you're asking me to leave Anna. She's the wan woman of the world for me, and I can't live without her now, I'm thinking.

CHRIS. You forgat all about her in one week out of port, Ay bet you!

BURKE. You don't know the like I am. Death itself wouldn't make me forget her. So let you not be making talk to me about leaving her. I'll not, and be damned to you! It won't be so bad for you as you'd make out at all. She'll be living here in the States, and her married to me. And you'd be seeing her often so – a sight more often than ever you saw her the fifteen years she was growing up in the West. It's quare you'd be the one to be making great trouble about her leaving you when you never laid eyes on her once in all them years.

CHRIS (*guiltily*). Ay taught it vas better Anna stay avay, grow up inland where she don't ever know ole davil, sea.

BURKE (*scornfully*). Is it blaming the sea for your troubles ye are again, God help you? Well, Anna knows it now. 'Twas in her blood, anyway.

CHRIS. And Ay don't vant she ever know no-good fallar on sea –

BURKE. She knows one now.

CHRIS (*banging the table with his fist – furiously*). Dat's yust it! Dat's yust what you are – no-good, sailor fallar! You tank Ay lat her life be made sorry by you like her mo'der's vas by me! No, Ay swear! She don't marry you if Ay gat kill you first!

BURKE (*looks at him a moment, in astonishment – then laughing uproariously*). Ho-ho! Glory be to God, it's bold talk you have for a stumpy runt of a man!

CHRIS (*threateningly*). Vell – you see!

BURKE (*with grinning defiance*). I'll see, surely! I'll see myself and
Anna married this day, I'm telling you! (*Then with contemptuous
exasperation.*) It's quare fool's blather you have about the sea
done this and the sea done that. You'd ought to be shamed to
be saying the like, and you an old sailor yourself. I'm after
hearing a lot of it from you and a lot more that Anna's told me
you do be saying to her, and I'm thinking it's a poor weak
thing you are, and not a man at all!

CHRIS (*darkly*). You see if Ay'm man – maybe quicker'n you
tank.

BURKE (*contemptuously*). Yerra, don't be boasting. I'm thinking
'tis out of your wits you've got with fright of the sea. You'd be
wishing Anna married to a farmer, she told me. That'd be a
swate match, surely. Would you have a fine girl the like of
Anna lying down at nights with a muddy scut stinking of pigs
and dung? Or would you have her tied for life to the like of
them skinny, shrivelled swabs does be working in cities?

CHRIS. Dat's lie, you fool!

BURKE. 'Tis not. 'Tis your own mad notions I'm after telling.
But you know the truth in your heart, if great fear of the sea
has made you a liar and coward itself. (*Pounding the table.*) The
sea's the only life for a man with guts in him isn't afraid of his
own shadow! 'Tis only on the sea he's free, and him roving the
face of the world, seeing all things, and not giving a damn for
saving up money, or stealing from his friends, or any of the
black tricks that a landlubber'd waste his life on. 'Twas yourself
knew it once, and you a bo'sun for years.

CHRIS (*sputtering with rage*). You vas crazy fool, Ay tal you!

BURKE. You've swallowed the anchor. The sea give you a clout
once knocked you down, and you're not man enough to get up
for another, but lie there for the rest of your life howling
bloody murder. (*Proudly.*) Isn't it myself the sea has nearly
drowned, and me battered and bate till I was that close to hell I
could hear the flames roaring, and never a groan out of me till
the sea gave up and it seeing the great strength and guts of a
man was in me?

CHRIS (*scornfully*). Yes, you vas hell of fallar, hear you tal it!

BURKE (*angrily*). You'll be calling me a liar once too often, me
old bucko! Wasn't the whole story of it and my picture itself in
the newspapers of Boston a week back? (*Looking* CHRIS *up and*

down belittlingly.) Sure, I'd like to see you in the best of your youth do the like of what I done in the storm and after. 'Tis a mad lunatic, screeching with fear, you'd be this minute!

CHRIS. Ho-ho! You vas young fool! In ole years when Ay was on windyammer, Ay vas through hundred storms vorse'n dat! Ships vas ships den – and men dat sail on dem vas real men. And now what you gat on steamers? You gat fallars on deck don't know ship from mudscow. (*With a meaning glance at* BURKE.) And below deck you gat fallars yust know how for shovel coal – might yust as vell vork on coal vagon ashore!

BURKE (*stung – angrily*). Is it casting insults at the men in the stokehole ye are, ye old ape? God stiffen you! Wan of them is worth any ten stock-fish-swilling Square-heads ever shipped on a windbag!

CHRIS (*his face working with rage, his hand going back to the sheath-knife on his hip*). Irish svine, you!

BURKE (*tauntingly*). Don't ye like the Irish, ye old baboon? 'Tis that you're needing in your family, I'm telling you – an Irishman and a man of the stokehole – to put guts in it so that you'll not be having grandchildren would be fearful cowards and jackasses the like of yourself!

CHRIS (*half-rising from his chair – in a voice choked with rage*). You look out!

BURKE (*watching him intently – a mocking smile on his lips*). And it's that you'll be having, no matter what you'll do to prevent; for Anna and me'll be married this day, and no old fool the like of you will stop us when I've made up my mind.

CHRIS (*with a hoarse cry*). You don't!

He throws himself at BURKE, *knife in hand, knocking his chair over backwards.* BURKE *springs to his feet quickly in time to meet the attack. He laughs with the pure love of battle. The old Swede is like a child in his hands.* BURKE *does not strike or mistreat him in any way, but simply twists his right hand behind his back and forces the knife from his fingers. He throws the knife into a far corner of the room – tauntingly.*

BURKE. Old men is getting childish shouldn't play with knives. (*Holding the struggling* CHRIS *at arm's length – with a sudden rush of anger, drawing back his fist.*) I've half a mind to hit you – a great clout will put sense in your square head. Kape off me now, I'm warning you! (*He gives* CHRIS *a push with the flat of his*

*hand which sends the old Swede staggering back against the cabin wall,
where he remains standing, panting heavily, his eyes fixed on* BURKE
*with hatred, as if he were only collecting his strength to rush at him
again. Warningly.*) Now don't be coming at me again, I'm saying,
or I'll flatten you on the floor with a blow, if 'tis Anna's father
you are itself! I've no patience left for you. (*Then with an amused
laugh.*) Well, 'tis a bold old man you are just the same, and I'd
never think it was in you to come tackling me alone. (*A shadow
crosses the cabin windows. Both men start.* ANNA *appears in the
doorway.*)

ANNA (*with pleased surprise as she sees* BURKE). Hallo, Mat. Are
you here already? I was down – (*She stops, looking from one to the
other, sensing immediately that something has happened.*) What's up?
(*Then noticing the overturned chair – in alarm.*) How'd that chair
get knocked over? (*Turning on* BURKE *reproachfully.*) You ain't
been fighting with him, Mat – after you promised?

BURKE (*his old self again*). I've not laid a hand on him, Anna. (*He
goes and picks up the chair, then turning on the still-questioning
ANNA – with a reassuring smile.*) Let you not be worried at all.
'Twas only a bit of an argument we was having to pass the time
till you'd come.

ANNA. It must have been some argument when you got to
throwing chairs. (*She turns on* CHRIS.) Why don't you say
something? What was it about?

CHRIS (*relaxing at last -- avoiding her eyes – sheepishly*). Ve vas
talking about ships and fallars on sea.

ANNA (*with a relieved smile*). Oh – the old stuff, eh?

BURKE (*suddenly seeming to come to a bold decision – with a defiant
grin at* CHRIS). He's not after telling you the whole of it. We
was arguing about you mostly.

ANNA (*with a frown*). About me?

BURKE. And we'll be finishing it out right here and now in your
presence if you're willing. (*He sits down at the left of the table.*)

ANNA (*uncertainly – looking from him to her father*). Sure. Tell me
what it's all about.

CHRIS (*advancing toward the table – protesting to* BURKE). No! You
don't do dat, you! You tal him you don't vant for hear him
talk, Anna.

ANNA. But I do. I want this cleared up.

CHRIS (*miserably afraid now*). Vell, not now, anyvay. You vas going ashore, yes? You ain't got time –

ANNA (*firmly*). Yes, right here and now. (*She turns to* BURKE.) You tell me, Mat, since he don't want to.

BURKE (*draws a deep breath – then plunges in boldly*). The whole of it's in a few words only. So's he'd make no mistake, and him hating the sight of me, I told him in his teeth I loved you. (*Passionately.*) And that's God truth, Anna, and well you know it!

CHRIS (*scornfully – forcing a laugh*). Ho-ho! He tal same tang to gel every port he go!

ANNA (*shrinking from her father with repulsion – resentfully*). Shut up, can't you? (*Then to* BURKE – *feelingly.*) I know it's true, Mat. I don't mind what he says.

BURKE (*humbly grateful*). God bless you!

ANNA. And then what?

BURKE. And then – (*Hesitatingly.*) And then I said – (*He looks at her pleadingly.*) I said I was sure – I told him I thought you have a bit of love for me, too. (*Passionately.*) Say you do, Anna! Let you not destroy me entirely, for the love of God! (*He grasps both her hands in his two.*)

ANNA (*deeply moved and troubled – forcing a trembling laugh*). So you told him that, Mat? No wonder he was mad. (*Forcing out the words.*) Well, maybe it's true, Mat. Maybe I do. I been thinking and thinking – I didn't want to, Mat, I'll own up to that – I tried to cut it out – but – (*She laughs helplessly.*) I guess I can't help it anyhow. So I guess I do, Mat. (*Then with a sudden joyous defiance.*) Sure I do! What's the use of kidding myself different? Sure I love you, Mat!

CHRIS (*with a cry of pain*). Anna! (*He sits crushed.*)

BURKE (*with a great depth of sincerity in his humble gratitude*). God be praised!

ANNA (*assertively*). And I ain't never loved a man in my life before, you can always believe that – no matter what happens.

BURKE (*goes over to her and puts his arms around her*). Sure I do be believing ivery word you iver said or iver will say. And 'tis you and me will be having a grand, beautiful life together to the end of our days!

He tries to kiss her. At first she turns away her head – then, overcome by a fierce impulse of passionate love, she takes his head in both her hands and holds his face close to hers, staring into his eyes. Then she kisses him full on the lips.

ANNA (*pushing him away from her – forcing a broken laugh*). Goodbye.

She walks to the doorway in rear – stands with her back toward them, looking out. Her shoulders quiver once or twice a if she were fighting back her sobs.

BURKE (*too in the seventh heaven of bliss to get any correct interpretation of her word – with a laugh*). Good-bye, is it? The divil you say! I'll be coming back at you in a second for more of the same! (*To CHRIS, who has quickened to instant attention at his daughter's good-bye, and has looked back at her with a stirring of foolish hope in his eyes.*) Now, me old bucko, what'll you be saying? You heard the words from her own lips. Confess I've bate you. Own up like a man when you're bate fair and square. And here's my hand to you – (*Holds out his hand.*) And let you take it and we'll shake and forget what's over and done, and be friends from this out.

CHRIS (*with implacable hatred*). Ay don't shake hands with you fallar – not vhile Ay live!

BURKE (*offended*). The back of my hand to you then, if that suits you better. (*Growling.*) 'Tis a rotten bad loser you are, divil mend you!

CHRIS. Ay don't lose – (*Trying to be scornful and self-convincing.*) Anna say she like you little bit, but you don't hear her say she marry you. Ay bet. (*At the sound of her name ANNA has turned round to them. Her face is composed and calm again, but it is the dead calm of despair.*)

BURKE (*scornfully*). No, and I wasn't hearing her say the sun is shining either.

CHRIS (*doggedly*). Dat's all right She don't say it, yust same.

ANNA (*quietly – coming forward to them*). No, I didn't say it, Mat.

CHRIS (*eagerly*). Dere! You hear!

BURKE (*misunderstanding her – with a grin*). You're waiting till you do be asked, you mane? Well, I'm asking you now. And we'll be married this day, with the help of God!

ANNA (*gently*). You heard what I said, Mat – after I kissed you?

BURKE (*alarmed by something in her manner*). No – I disremember.

ANNA. I said good-bye. (*Her voice trembling.*) That kiss was for good-bye, Mat.

BURKE (*terrified*). What d'you mane?

ANNA. I can't marry you, Mat – and we've said good-bye. That's all.

CHRIS (*unable to hold back his exultation*). Ay know it! Ay know dat vas so!

BURKE (*jumping to his feet – unable to believe his ears*). Anna! Is it making game of me you'd be? 'Tis a quare time to joke with me, and don't be doing it, for the love of God.

ANNA (*looking him in the eyes – steadily*). D'you think I'd kid you now? No, I'm not joking, Mat. I mean what I said.

BURKE. Ye don't! Ye can't! 'Tis mad you are, I'm telling you!

ANNA (*fixedly*). No, I'm not.

BURKE (*desperately*). But what's come over you so sudden? You was saying you loved me –

ANNA. I'll say that as often as you want me to. It's true.

BURKE (*bewildered*). Then why – what, in the divil's name – Oh, God help me, I can't make head or tail to it at all!

ANNA. Because it's the best way out I can figure, Mat. (*Her voice catching.*) I been thinking it over and thinking it over day and night all week. Don't think it ain't hard on me, too, Mat.

BURKE. For the love of God, tell me then, what is it that's preventing you wedding me when the two of us has love? (*Suddenly getting an idea and pointing at* CHRIS – *with exasperation.*) Is it giving heed to the like of that old fool ye are, and him hating me and filling your ears full of bloody lies against me?

CHRIS (*getting to his feet – raging triumphantly before* ANNA *has a chance to get in a word*). Yes, Anna believe me, not you! She know her old fa'der don't lie like you.

ANNA (*turning on her father angrily*). You sit down, d'you hear? Where do you come in butting in and making things worse? You're like a devil, you are! (*Harshly.*) Good Lord, and I was beginning to like you, beginning to forget all I've got held up against you!

CHRIS (*crushed – feebly*). You ain't got nutting for hold against me, Anna.

ANNA. Ain't I yust! Well, lemme tell you – (*She glances at* BURKE *and stops abruptly.*) Say, Mat, I'm s'prised at you. You didn't think anything he'd said –

BURKE (*glumly*). Sure, what else would it be?

ANNA. Think I've ever paid any attention to all his crazy bull? Gee, you must take me for a five-year-old kid.

BURKE (*puzzled and beginning to be irritated at her too*). I don't know how to take you, with your saying this one minute and that the next.

ANNA. Well, he has nothing to do with it.

BURKE. Then what is it has? Tell me, and don't keep me waiting and sweating blood.

ANNA (*resolutely*). I can't tell you – and I won't. I got a good reason – and that's all you need to know. I can't marry you, that's all there is to it. (*Distractedly.*) So, for Gawd's sake, let's talk of something else.

BURKE. I'll not! (*Then fearfully.*) Is it married to some one else you are – in the West maybe?

ANNA (*vehemently*). I should say not.

BURKE (*regaining his courage*). To the divil with all other reasons then. They don't matter with me at all. (*He gets to his feet confidently, assuming a masterful tone.*) I'm thinking you're the like of them women can't make up their mind till they're drove to it. Well, then, I'll make up your mind for you bloody quick. (*He takes her by the arms, grinning to soften his serious bullying.*) We've had enough of talk! Let you be going into your room now and be dressing in your best and we'll be going ashore.

CHRIS (*aroused – angrily*). No, py God, she don't do that! (*Takes hold of her arm.*)

ANNA (*who has listened to* BURKE *in astonishment. She draws away from him, instinctively repelled by his tone, but not exactly sure if he is serious or not – a trace of resentment in her voice*). Say, where do you get that stuff?

BURKE (*imperiously*). Never mind, now! Let you go get dressed, I'm saying. (*Then turning to* CHRIS.) We'll be seeing who'll win in the end – me or you.

CHRIS (*to* ANNA – *also in the authoritative tone*). You stay right here, Anna, you hear.

ANNA *stands looking from one to the other of them as if she thought they had both gone crazy. Then the expression of her face freezes into the hardened sneer of her experience.*

BURKE (*violently*). She'll not! She'll do what I say! You've had your hold on her long enough. It's my turn now.

ANNA (*with a hard laugh*). Your turn? Say, what am I, anyway?

BURKE. 'Tis not what you are 'tis what you're going to be this day – and that's wedded to me before night comes. Hurry up now with your dressing.

CHRIS (*commandingly*). You don't do one tang he say, Anna!

ANNA *laughs mockingly.*

BURKE. She will, so!

CHRIS. Ay tal you she don't! Ay'm her fa'der.

BURKE. She will in spite of you. She's taking my orders from this out, not yours.

ANNA (*laughing again*). Orders is good!

BURKE (*turning to her impatiently*). Hurry up now, and shake a leg. We've no time to be wasting. (*Irritated as she doesn't move.*) Do you hear what I'm telling you?

CHRIS. You stay dere, Anna!

ANNA (*at the end of her patience – blazing out at them passionately*). You can go to hell, both of you! (*There is something in her tone that makes them forget their quarrel and turn to her in a stunned amazement.* ANNA *laughs wildly.*) You're just like all the rest of them – you two! Gawd, you'd think I was a piece of furniture! I'll show you! Sit down now! (*As they hesitate – furiously.*) Sit down and let me talk for a minute. You're all wrong, see? Listen to me! I'm going to tell you something – and then I'm going to beat it. (*To* BURKE – *with a harsh laugh.*) I'm going to tell you a funny story, so pay attention. (*Pointing to* CHRIS.) I've been meaning to turn it loose on him every time he'd get my goat with his bull about keeping me safe inland. I wasn't going

to tell you, but you've forced me into it. What's the dif? It's all
wrong anyway, and you might as well get cured that way as any
other. (*With hard mocking.*) Only don't forget what you said a
minute ago about it not mattering to you what other reason I
got so long as I wasn't married to no one else.

BURKE (*manfully*). That's my word, and I'll stick to it!

ANNA (*laughing bitterly*). What a chance! You make me laugh,
honest! Want to bet you will? Wait'n' see! (*She stands at the table
rear, looking from one to the other of the two men with her hard,
mocking smile. Then she begins, fighting to control her emotion and
speak calmly.*) First thing is, I want to tell you two guys
something. You was going on's if one of you had got to own
me. But nobody owns me, see? – 'cepting myself. I'll do what I
please, and no man, I don't give a hoot who he is, can tell me
what to do! I ain't asking either of you for a living. I can make
it myself – one way or other. I'm my own boss. So put that in
your pipe and smoke it! You and your orders!

BURKE (*protestingly*). I wasn't meaning it that way at all and well
you know it. You've no call to be raising this rumpus with me.
(*Pointing to* CHRIS.) 'Tis him you've a right –

ANNA. I'm coming to him. But you – you did mean it that way,
too. You sounded – yust like all the rest. (*Hysterically.*) But,
damn it, shut up! Let me talk for a change!

BURKE. 'Tis quare, rough talk, that – for a dacent girl the like
of you!

ANNA (*with a hard laugh*). Decent? Who told you I was? (CHRIS
*is sitting with bowed shoulders, his head in his hands. She leans over in
exasperation and shakes him violently by the shoulder.*) Don't go to
sleep, Old Man! Listen here, I'm talking to you now!

CHRIS (*straightening up and looking about as if he were seeking a way
to escape – with frightened foreboding in his voice*). Ay don't vant for
hear it. You vas going out of head, Ay tank, Anna.

ANNA (*violently*). Well, living with you is enough to drive anyone
off their nut. Your bunk about the farm being so fine! Didn't I
write you year after year how rotten it was and what a dirty
slave them cousins made of me? What'd you care? Nothing!
Not even enough to come out and see me! That crazy bull
about wanting to keep me away from the sea don't go down
with me! You yust didn't want to be bothered with me! You're
like all the rest of 'em!

CHRIS (*feebly*). Anna! It ain't so –

ANNA (*not heeding his interruption – revengefully*). But one thing I
never wrote you. It was one of them cousins that you think is
such nice people – the youngest son – Paul – that started me
wrong. (*Loudly.*) It wasn't none of my fault. I hated him worse'n
hell, and he knew it. But he was big and strong – (*Pointing to
BURKE.*) – like you!

BURKE (*half-springing to his feet – his fists clenched*). God blarst it!
(*He sinks slowly back in his chair again, the knuckles showing white on
his clenched hands, his face tense with the effort to suppress his grief
and rage.*)

CHRIS (*in a cry of horrified pain*). Anna!

ANNA (*to him – seeming not to have heard their interruptions*). That
was why I run away from the farm. That was what made me
get a yob as nurse girl in St Paul. (*With a hard, mocking laugh.*)
And you think that was a nice yob for a girl, too, don't you?
(*Sarcastically.*) With all them nice inland fellers yust looking for
a chance to marry me, I s'pose. Marry me? What a chance!
They wasn't looking for marrying. (*As BURKE lets a groan of
fury escape him – desperately.*) I'm owning up to everything fair
and square. I was caged in, I tell you – yust like in yail – taking
care of other people's kids – listening to 'em bawling and crying
day and night – when I wanted to be out – and I was lonesome
as hell! (*With a sudden weariness in her voice.*) So I give up finally.
What was the use? (*She stops and looks at the two men. Both are
motionless and silent. CHRIS seems in a stupor of despair, his house of
cards fallen about him. BURKE's face is livid with the rage that is
eating him up, but he is too stunned and bewildered yet to find a vent
for it. The condemnation she feels in their silence goads ANNA into a
harsh, strident defiance.*) You don't say nothing – either of you –
but I know what you're thinking. You're like all the rest! (*To
CHRIS – furiously.*) And who's to blame for it, me or you? If
you'd ever acted like a man – if you'd ever been a regular
father and had me with you – maybe things would be different!

CHRIS (*in agony*). Don't talk dat vay, Anna! Ay go crazy! Ay von't
listen! (*Puts his hands over his ears.*)

ANNA (*infuriated by his action – stridently*). You will listen though!
(*She leans over and pulls his hands from his ears – with hysterical
rage.*) You – keeping me safe inland – I wasn't no nurse girl the
last two years – I lied when I wrote you – I was in a house,
that's what – yes, that kind of a house – the kind sailors like

you and Mat goes to in port – and your nice inland men, too –
and all men, God damn 'em! I hate 'em! Hate 'em! (*She breaks
into hysterical sobbing, throwing herself into the chair and hiding her
face in her hands on the table. The two men have sprung to their feet.*)

CHRIS (*whimpering like a child*). Anna! Anna! It's lie! It's lie! (*He
stands wringing his hands together and begins to weep.*)

BURKE (*his whole great body tense like a spring – dully and gropingly*).
So that's what's in it!

ANNA (*raising her head at the sound of his voice – with extreme
mocking bitterness*). I s'pose you remember your promise, Mat?
No other reason was to count with you so long as I wasn't
married already. So I s'pose you want me to get dressed and go
ashore, don't you? (*She laughs.*) Yes, you do!

BURKE (*on the verge of his outbreak – stammering*). God stiffen you!

ANNA (*trying to keep up her hard, bitter tone, but gradually letting a
note of pitiful pleading creep in*). I s'pose if I tried to tell you I
wasn't – that – no more you'd believe me, wouldn't you? Yes,
you would! And if I told you that yust getting out in this barge,
and being on the sea had changed me and made me feel
different about things, 's if all I'd been through wasn't me and
didn't count and was yust like it never happened – you'd laugh,
wouldn't you? And you'd die laughing sure if I said that
meeting you that funny way that night in the fog, and
afterwards seeing that you was straight goods stuck on me, had
got me to thinking for the first time, and I sized you up as
different from the ones on land as water is from mud – and
that was why I got stuck on you, too. I wanted to marry you
and fool you, but I couldn't. Don't you see how I'd changed? I
couldn't marry you with you believing a lie – and I was shamed
to tell you the truth – till the both of you forced my hand, and
I seen you was the same as all the rest. And now, give me a
bawling out and beat it, like I can tell you're going to. (*She stops,
looking at* BURKE. *He is silent, his face averted, his features
beginning to work with fury. She pleads passionately.*) Will you
believe it if I tell you that loving you has made me – clean? It's
the straight goods, honest! (*Then as he doesn't reply – bitterly.*)
Like hell you will! You're like all the rest!

BURKE (*blazing out – turning on her in a perfect frenzy of rage – his
voice trembling with passion*). The rest, is it? God's curse on you!
Clane, is it? You slut, you, I'll be killing you now! (*He picks up
the chair on which he has been sitting, and, swinging it high over his*

shoulder, springs toward her. CHRIS *rushes forward with a cry of alarm, trying to ward off the blow from his daughter.* ANNA *looks up into* BURKE's *eyes with the fearlessness of despair.* BURKE *checks himself, the chair held in the air.*)

CHRIS (*wildly*). Stop, you crazy fool! You vant for murder her?

ANNA (*pushing her father away brusquely, her eyes still holding* BURKE's). Keep out of this, you! (*To* BURKE – *dully.*) Well, ain't you got the nerve to do it? Go ahead! I'll be thankful to you, honest. I'm sick of the whole game.

BURKE (*throwing the chair away into a corner of the room – helplessly*). I can't do it, God help me, and your two eyes looking at me. (*Furiously.*) Though I do be thinking I'd have a good right to smash your skull like a rotten egg. Was there iver a woman in the world had the rottenness in her that you have, and was there iver a man the like of me was made the fool of the world, and me thinking thoughts about you, and having great love for you, and dreaming dreams of the fine life we'd have when we'd be wedded! (*His voice high-pitched in a lamentation that is like a keen.*) Yerra, God help me! I'm destroyed entirely and my heart is broken in bits! I'm asking God Himself, was it for this He'd have me roaming the earth since I was a lad only, to come to black shame in the end, where I'd be giving a power of love to a woman is the same as others you'd meet in any hooker-shanty in port, with red gowns on them and paint on their grinning mugs, would be sleeping with any man for a dollar or two!

ANNA (*in a scream*). Don't, Mat! For Gawd's sake! (*Then raging and pounding on the table with her hands.*) Get out of here! Leave me alone! Get out of here!

BURKE (*his anger rushing back on him*). I'll be going, surely! And I'll be drinking sloos of whisky will wash that black kiss of yours off my lips; and I'll be getting dead rotten drunk so I'll not remember if 'twas iver born you was at all; and I'll be shipping away on some boat will take me to the other end of the world where I'll never see your face again! (*He turns toward the door.*)

CHRIS (*who has been standing in a stupor – suddenly grasping* BURKE *by the arm – stupidly*). No, you don't go. Ay tank maybe it's better Anna marry you now.

BURKE (*shaking* CHRIS *off – furiously*). Lave go of me, ye old ape! Marry her, is it? I'd see her roasting in hell first! I'm shipping away out of this, I'm telling you! (*Pointing to* ANNA – *passionately.*) And my curse on you and the curse of Almighty

God and all the Saints! You've destroyed me this day, and may you lie awake in the long nights, tormented with thoughts of Mat Burke and the great wrong you've done him!

ANNA (*in anguish*). Mat! (*But he turns without another word and strides out of the doorway. ANNA looks after him wildly, starts to run after him, then hides her face in her outstretched arms, sobbing. CHRIS stands in a stupor, staring at the floor.*)

CHRIS (*after a pause, dully*). Ay tank Ay go ashore, too.

ANNA (*looking up, wildly*). Not after him! Let him go! Don't you dare –

CHRIS (*sombrely*). Ay go for gat drink.

ANNA (*with a harsh laugh*). So I'm driving you to drink, too, eh? I s'pose you want to get drunk so's you can forget – like him?

CHRIS (*bursting out angrily*). Yes, Ay vant! You tank Ay like hear dem tangs. (*Breaking down – weeping.*) Ay tank you vasn't dat kind of gel, Anna.

ANNA (*mockingly*). And I s'pose you want me to beat it, don't you? You don't want me here disgracing you, I s'pose?

CHRIS. No, you stay here! (*Goes over and pats her on the shoulder, the tears running down his face.*) Ain't your fault, Anna, Ay know dat. (*She looks up at him, softened. He bursts into rage.*) It's dat ole davil, sea, do this to me! (*He shakes his fist at the door.*) It's her dirty tricks! It vas all right on barge with yust you and me. Den she bring dat Irish fallar in fog, she make you like him, she make you fight with me all time! If dat Irish fallar don't never come, you don't never tal me dem tangs, Ay don't never know, and everytang's all right. (*He shakes his fist again.*) Dirty ole davil!

ANNA (*with spent weariness*). Oh, what's the use? Go on ashore and get drunk.

CHRIS (*goes into room on left and gets his cap. He goes to the door, silent and stupid – then turns*). You vait here, Anna?

ANNA (*dully*). Maybe – and maybe not. Maybe I'll get drunk, too. Maybe I'll – But what the hell do you care what I do? Go on and beat it. (*CHRIS turns stupidly and goes out. ANNA sits at the table, staring straight in front of her.*)

The curtain falls.

ACT FOUR

Same as Act Three, about nine o'clock of a foggy night two days later. The whistles of steamers in the harbour can be heard. The cabin is lighted by a small lamp on the table. A suitcase stands in the middle of the floor.

ANNA *is sitting in the rocking-chair. She wears a hat, is all dressed up as in Act One. Her face is pale, looks terribly tired and worn, as if the two days just past had been ones of suffering and sleepless nights. She stares before her despondently, her chin in her hands. There is a timid knock on the door in rear.* ANNA *jumps to her feet with a startled exclamation and looks toward the door with an expression of mingled hope and fear.*

ANNA (*faintly*). Come in. (*Then summoning her courage – more resolutely.*) Come in. (*The door is opened and* CHRIS *appears in the doorway. He is in a very bleary, bedraggled condition, suffering from the after-effects of his drink. A tin pail full of foaming beer is in his hand. He comes forward, his eyes avoiding* ANNA's. *He mutters stupidly, 'It's foggy.'*)

ANNA (*looking him over with contempt*). So you come back at last, did you? You're a fine-looking sight! (*Then jeeringly.*) I thought you'd beaten it for good on account of the disgrace I'd brought on you.

CHRIS (*wincing – faintly*). Don't say dat, Anna, please! (*He sits in a chair by the table, setting down the can of beer, holding his head in his hands.*)

ANNA (*looks at him with a certain sympathy*). What's the trouble? Feeling sick?

CHRIS (*dully*). Inside my head feel sick.

ANNA. Well, what d'you expect after being soused for two days? (*Resentfully.*) It serves you right. A fine thing – you leaving me alone on this barge all that time!

CHRIS (*humbly*). Ay'm sorry, Anna.

ANNA (*scornfully*). Sorry!

CHRIS. But Ay'm not sick inside head vay you mean. Ay'm sick from tank too much about you, about me.

ANNA. And how about me? D'you suppose I ain't been thinking too?

CHRIS. Ay'm sorry, Anna (*He sees her bag and gives a start.*) You pack your bag, Anna? You vas going –

ANNA (*forcibly*). Yes, I was going right back to what you think.

CHRIS. Anna!

ANNA. I went ashore to get a train for New York. I'd been waiting and waiting till I was sick of it. Then I changed my mind and decided not to go today. But I'm going first thing tomorrow, so it'll all be the same in the end.

CHRIS (*raising his head – pleadingly*). No, you never do dat, Anna!

ANNA (*with a sneer*). Why not, I'd like to know?

CHRIS. You don't never gat to do – dat way – no more, Ay tal you. Ay fix dat up all right.

ANNA (*suspiciously*). Fix what up?

CHRIS (*not seeming to have heard her question – sadly*). You vas vaiting, you say? You vasn't vaiting for me, Ay bet.

ANNA (*callously*). You'd win.

CHRIS. For dat Irish fallar?

ANNA (*defiantly*). Yes – if you want to know! (*Then with a forlorn laugh.*) If he did come back it'd only be 'cause he wanted to beat me up or kill me, I suppose. But even if he did, I'd rather have him come than not show up at all. I wouldn't care what he did.

CHRIS. Ay guess it's true you vas in love with him all right.

ANNA. You guess!

CHRIS (*turning to her earnestly*). And Ay'm sorry for you like hell he don't come, Anna!

ANNA (*softened*). Seems to me you've changed your tune a lot.

CHRIS. Ay've been tanking, and Ay guess it vas all my fault – all bad tangs dat happen to you. (*Pleadingly.*) You try for not hate me, Anna. Ay'm crazy ole fool, dat's all.

ANNA. Who said I hated you?

CHRIS. Ay'm sorry for everytang Ay do wrong for you, Anna. Ay vant for you be happy all rest of your life for make up! It make you happy marry dat Irish fallar, Ay vant it, too.

ANNA (*dully*). Well, there ain't no chance. But I'm glad you think different about it, anyway.

CHRIS (*supplicatingly*). And you tank – maybe – you forgive me sometime?

ANNA (*with a wan smile*). I'll forgive you right now.

CHRIS (*seizing her hand and kissing it – brokenly*). Anna lilla! Anna lilla!

ANNA (*touched but a bit embarrassed*). Don't bawl about it. There ain't nothing to forgive, anyway. It ain't your fault, and it ain't mine, and it ain't his neither. We're all poor nuts, and things happen, and we yust get mixed in wrong, that's all.

CHRIS (*eagerly*). You say right tang, Anna, py golly! It ain't nobody's fault! (*Shaking his fist.*) It's dat ole davil, sea!

ANNA (*with an exasperated laugh*). Gee, won't you ever can that stuff? (CHRIS *relapses into injured silence. After a pause* ANNA *continues curiously.*) You said a minute ago you'd fixed something up – about me. What was it?

CHRIS (*after a hesitating pause*). Ay'm shipping avay on sea again, Anna.

ANNA (*astounded*). You're – what?

CHRIS. Ay sign on steamer sail tomorrow. Ay gat my ole yob – bos'n. (ANNA *stares at him. As he goes on, a bitter smile comes over her face*). Ay tank dat's best tang for you. Ay only bring you bad luck, Ay tank. Ay make your mo'der's life sorry. Ay don't vant make yours dat way, but Ay do yust same. Dat ole davil, sea, she make me Yonah man ain't no good for nobody. And Ay tank now it ain't no use fight with sea. No man dat live going to beat her, py yingo!

ANNA (*with a laugh of helpless bitterness*). So that's how you've fixed me, is it?

CHRIS. Yes, Ay tank if dat ole davil gat me back she leave you alone den.

ANNA (*bitterly*). But, for Gawd's sake, don't you see, you're doing the same thing you've always done? Don't you see – (*But she sees the look of obsessed stubbornness on her father's face and gives it up helplessly*). But what's the use of talking. You ain't right, that's what. I'll never blame you for nothing no more. But how you could figure out that was fixing me –

CHRIS. Dat ain't all. Ay gat dem fallars in steamship office to pay you all money coming to me every month vhile Ay'm avay.

ANNA (with a hard laugh). Thanks. But I guess I won't be hard up for no small change.

CHRIS (hurt – humbly). It ain't much, Ay know, but it's plenty for keep you so you never gat go back –

ANNA (shortly). Shut up, will you! We'll talk about it later, see?

CHRIS (after a pause – ingratiatingly). You like Ay go ashore look for dat Irish fallar, Anna?

ANNA (angrily). Not much! Think I want to drag him back?

CHRIS (after a pause – uncomfortably). Py golly, dat booze don't go vell. Give me fever, Ay tank. Ay feel hot like hell. (He takes off his coat and lets it drop on the floor. There is a loud thud.)

ANNA (with a start). What you got in your pocket, for Pete's sake – a ton of lead? (She reaches down, takes the coat and pulls out a revolver – looks from it to him in amazement.) A gun? What were you doing with this?

CHRIS (sheepishly). Ay forgat. Ain't nutting. Ain't loaded, anyway.

ANNA (breaking it open to make sure – then closing it again – looking at him suspiciously). That ain't telling me why you got it?

CHRIS (sheepishly). Ay'm ole fool. Ay gat it ven Ay go ashore first. Ay tank den it's all fault of dat Irish fallar.

ANNA (with a shudder). Say, you're crazier than I thought. I never dreamt you'd go that far.

CHRIS (quickly). Ay don't. Ay gat better sense right avay. Ay don't never buy bullets even. It ain't his fault, Ay know.

ANA (still suspicious of him). Well, I'll take care of this for a while, loaded or not. (She puts it in the drawer of table and closes the drawer.)

CHRIS (placatingly). Throw it overboard if you vant. Ay don't care. (Then after a pause.) Py golly, Ay tank Ay go lie down. Ay feel sick. (ANNA takes a magazine from the table. CHRIS hesitates by her chair.) Ve talk again before Ay go, yes?

ANNA (dully). Where's this ship going to?

CHRIS. Cape Town, Dat's in South Africa. She's British steamer called Londonderry. (He stands hesitatingly – finally blurts out.) Anna – you forgive me sure?

ANNA (*wearily*). Sure I do. You ain't to blame. You're yust – what you are – like me.

CHRIS (*pleadingly*). Den – you lat me kiss you again once?

ANNA (*raising her face – forcing a wan smile*). Sure. No hard feelings.

CHRIS (*kisses her – brokenly*). Anna lilla! Ay – (*He fights for words to express himself, but finds none – miserably – with a sob.*) Ay can't say it. Good night, Anna.

ANNA. Good night. (*He picks up the can of beer and goes slowly into the room on left, his shoulders bowed, his head sunk forward dejectedly. He closes the door after him. ANNA turns over the pages of the magazine, trying desperately to banish her thoughts by looking at the pictures. This fails to distract her, and flinging the magazine back on the table, she springs to her feet and walks about the cabin distractedly, clenching and unclenching her hands. She speaks aloud to herself in a tense, trembling voice.*) Gawd, I can't stand this much longer! What am I waiting for anyway? – like a damn fool! (*She laughs helplessly, then checks herself abruptly, as she hears the sound of heavy footsteps on the deck outside. She appears to recognize these and her face lights up with joy She gasps.*) Mat!

A strange terror seems suddenly to seize her. She rushes to the table, takes the revolver out of drawer, and crouches down in the corner, left, behind the cupboard. A moment later the door is flung open and MAT BURKE appears in the doorway. He is in bad shape – his clothes torn and dirty, covered with sawdust as if he had been grovelling or sleeping on bar-room floors. There is a red bruise on his forehead over one of his eyes, another over his cheekbone, his knuckles are skinned and raw – plain evidence of the fighting he has been through on his 'bat'. His eyes are bloodshot and heavy-lidded, his face has a bloated look. But beyond these appearances – the results of heavy drinking – there is an expression in his eyes of wild mental turmoil, of impotent animal rage baffled by its own abject misery.

BURKE (*peers blinkingly about the cabin – hoarsely*). Let you not be hiding from me, whoever's here – though 'tis well you know I'd have a right to come back and murder you. (*He stops to listen. Hearing no sound, he closes the door behind him and comes forward to the table. He throws himself into the rocking-chair – despondently.*) There's no one here, I'm thinking, and 'tis a great fool I am to be coming. (*With a sort of dumb, uncomprehending anguish.*) Yerra, Mat Burke, 'tis a great jackass you've become and what's got into you at all, at all? She's gone out of this long ago, I'm telling you, and you'll never see her face again. (ANNA *stands up, hesitating, struggling between joy and fear.* BURKE'*s eyes fall on* ANNA'*s bag. He leans over to examine it.*) What's this? (*Joyfully.*) It's hers. She's not gone! But where is she? Ashore? (*Darkly.*) What would she be doing ashore on this rotten night. (*His face suddenly convulsed with grief and rage.*) 'Tis that, is it? Oh, God's curse on her! (*Raging.*) I'll wait till she comes and choke her dirty life out.

ANNA *starts, her face grows hard. She steps into the room, the revolver in her right hand by her side.*

ANNA (*in a cold, hard tone*). What are you doing here?

BURKE (*wheeling about with a terrified gasp*). Glory be to God! (*They remain motionless and silent for a moment, holding each other's eyes.*)

ANNA (*in the same hard voice*). Well, can't you talk?

BURKE (*trying to fall into an easy, careless tone*). You've a year's growth scared out of me, coming at me so sudden and me thinking I was alone.

ANNA. You've got your nerve butting in here without knocking or nothing. What d'you want?

BURKE (*airily*). Oh, nothing much. I was wanting to have a last word with you, that's all. (*He moves a step toward her.*)

ANNA (*sharply – raising the revolver in her hand*). Careful now! Don't try getting too close. I heard what you said you'd do to me.

BURKE (*noticing the revolver for the first time*). Is it murdering me you'd be now, God forgive you? (*Then with a contemptuous laugh.*) Or is it thinking I'd be frightened by that old tin whistle? (*He walks straight for her.*)

ANNA (*wildly*). Look out, I tell you!

BURKE (*who has come so close that the revolver is almost touching his chest*). Let you shoot, then! (*Then with sudden wild grief.*) Let you shoot, 1 m saying, and be done with it! Let you end me with a shot and I'll be thanking you, for it's a rotten dog's life I've lived the past two days since I've known what you are, till I'm after wishing I was never born at all!

ANNA (*overcome – letting the revolver drop to the floor, as if her fingers had no strength to hold it – hysterically*). What d'you want coming here? Why don't you beat it? Go on! (*She passes him and sinks down in the rocking-chair.*)

BURKE (*following her – mournfully*). 'Tis right you'd be asking why did I come. (*Then angrily.*) 'Tis because 'tis a great weak fool of the world I am, and me tormented with the wickedness you'd told of yourself, and drinking oceans of booze that'd make me forget. Forget? Divil a word I'd forget, and your face grinning always in front of my eyes, awake or asleep, till I do be thinking a madhouse is the proper place for me.

ANNA (*glancing at his hands and face – scornfully*). You look like you ought to be put away some place. Wonder you wasn't pulled in. You been scrapping, too, ain't you?

BURKE. I have – with every scut would take off his coat to me! (*Fiercely.*) And each time I'd be hitting one a clout in the mug, it wasn't his face I'd be seeing at all, but yours, and me wanting to drive you a blow would knock you out of this world where I wouldn't be seeing or thinking more of you.

ANNA (*her lips trembling pitifully*). Thanks!

BURKE (*walking up and down – distractedly*). That's right, make game of me! Oh, I'm a great coward surely, to be coming back to speak with you at all. You've a right to laugh at me.

ANNA. I ain't laughing at you, Mat.

BURKE (*unheeding*). You to be what you are, and me to be Mat Burke, and me to be drove back to look at you again! 'Tis black shame is on me!

ANNA (*resentfully*). Then get out. No one's holding you!

BURKE (*bewilderedly*). And me to listen to that talk from a woman like you and be frightened to close her mouth with a slap! Oh, God help me, I'm a yellow coward for all men to spit at! (*Then furiously.*) But I'll not be getting out of this till I've had me word. (*Raising his fist threateningly.*) And let you look out how you'd drive me! (*Letting his fist fall helplessly.*) Don't be angry now! I'm raving like a real lunatic, I'm thinking, and the sorrow you put on me has my brains drownded in grief. (*Suddenly bending down to her and grasping her arm intensely.*) Tell me it's a lie, I'm saying! That's what I'm after coming to hear you say.

ANNA (*dully*). A lie? What?

BURKE (*with passionate entreaty*). All the badness you told me two days back. Sure it must be a lie! You was only making game of me, wasn't you? Tell me 'twas a lie, Anna, and I'll be saying prayers of thanks on my two knees to the Almighty God!

ANNA (*terribly shaken – faintly*). I can't, Mat. (*As he turns away – imploringly.*) Oh, Mat, won't you see that no matter what I was I ain't that any more? Why, listen! I packed up my bag this afternoon and went ashore. I'd been waiting here all alone for two days, thinking maybe you'd come back – thinking maybe you'd think over all I'd said – and maybe – oh, I don't know what I was hoping! But I was afraid to even go out of the cabin for a second, honest – afraid you might come and not find me here. Then I gave up hope when you didn't show up and I went to the railroad station. I was going to New York. I was going back –

BURKE (*hoarsely*). God's curse on you!

ANNA. Listen, Mat! You hadn't come, and I'd gave up hope. But – in the station – I couldn't go. I'd bought my ticket and everything. (*She takes the ticket from her dress and tries to hold it before his eyes.*) But I got to thinking about you – and I couldn't take the train – I couldn't! So I come back here – to wait some more. Oh, Mat, don't you see I've changed? Can't you forgive what's dead and gone – and forget it?

BURKE (*turning on her – overcome by rage again*). Forget, is it? I'll not forget till my dying day, I'm telling you, and me tormented with thoughts. (*In a frenzy.*) Oh, I'm wishing I had wan of them fornenst me this minute and I'd beat him with my fists till he'd be a bloody corpse! I'm wishing the whole lot of them will roast in hell till the Judgement Day – and yourself along with them, for you're as bad as they are.

ANNA (*shuddering*). Mat! (*Then after a pause – in a voice of dead, stony calm.*) Well, you've had your say. Now you better beat it.

BURKE (*starts slowly for the door – hesitates – then after a pause*). And what'll you be doing?

ANNA. What difference does it make to you?

BURKE. I'm asking you!

ANNA (*in the same tone*). My bag's packed and I got my ticket. I'll go to New York tomorrow.

BURKE (*helplessly*). You mean – you'll be doing the same again?

ANNA (*stonily*). Yes.

BURKE (*in anguish*). You'll not! Don't torment me with that talk! 'Tis a she-devil you are sent to drive me mad entirely!

ANNA (*her voice breaking*). Oh, for Gawd's sake, Mat, leave me alone! Go away! Don't you see I'm licked? Why d'you want to keep on kicking me?

BURKE (*indignantly*). And don't you deserve the worst I'd say, God forgive you?

ANNA. All right. Maybe I do. But don't rub it in. Why ain't you done what you said you was going to? Why ain't you got that ship was going to take you to the other side of the earth where you'd never see me again?

BURKE. I have.

ANNA (*startled*). What – then you're going – honest?

BURKE. I signed on today at noon, drunk as I was – and she's sailing tomorrow.

ANNA. And where's she going to?

BURKE. Cape Town.

ANNA (*the memory of having heard that name a little while before coming to her – with a start, confusedly*). Cape Town? Where's that? Far away?

BURKE. 'Tis at the end of Africa. That's far for you.

ANNA (*forcing a laugh*). You're keeping your word all right, ain't you? (*After a slight pause – curiously.*) What's the boat's name?

BURKE. The *Londonderry*.

ANNA (*it suddenly comes to her that this is the same ship her father is sailing on*). The *Londonderry*! It's the same – oh, this is too much! (*With wild, ironical laughter.*) Ha-ha-ha!

BURKE. What's up with you now!

ANNA. Ha-ha-ha! It's funny, funny! I'll die laughing!

BURKE (*irritated*). Laughing at what?

ANNA. It's a secret. You'll know soon enough. It's funny. (*Controlling herself – after a pause – cynically.*) What kind of a place is this Cape Town? Plenty of dames there, I suppose?

BURKE. To hell with them! That I may never see another woman to my dying hour!

ANNA. That's what you say now, but I'll bet by the time you get
there you'll have forgot all about me and start in talking the
same old bull you talked to me to the first one you meet.

BURKE (*offended*). I'll not, then! God mend you, is it making me
out to be the like of yourself you are, and you taking up with
this one and that all the years of your life?

ANNA (*angrily assertive*). Yes, that's yust what I do mean! You
been doing the same thing all your life, picking up a new girl
in every port. How're you any better than I was?

BURKE (*thoroughly exasperated*). Is it no shame you have at all?
I'm a fool to be wasting talk on you and you hardened in
badness. I'll go out of this and lave you alone for ever. (*He
starts for the door – then stops to turn on her furiously.*) And I
suppose 'tis the same lies you told them all before that you told
to me?

ANNA (*indignantly*). That's a lie! I never did!

BURKE (*miserably*). You'd be saying that, anyway.

ANNA (*forcibly, with growing intensity*). Are you trying to accuse
me – of being in love – really in love – with them?

BURKE. I'm thinking you were, surely.

ANNA (*furiously, as if this were the last insult – advancing on him
threateningly*). You mutt, you! I've stood enough from you.
Don't you dare. (*With scornful bitterness.*) Love 'em! Oh, my
Gawd! You damn thick-head! Love 'em? (*Savagely.*) I hated 'em,
I tell you! Hated 'em, hated 'em, hated 'em! And may Gawd
strike me dead this minute and my mother, too, if she was
alive, if I ain't telling you the honest truth!

BURKE (*immensely pleased by her vehemence – a light beginning to
break over his face – but still uncertain, torn between doubt and the
desire to believe – helplessly*). If I could only be believing you now!

ANNA (*distractedly*). Oh, what's the use? What's the use of me
talking? What's the use of anything? (*Pleading.*) Oh, Mat, you
mustn't think that for a second! You mustn't! Think all the
other bad about me you want to, and I won't kick, 'cause you've
a right to. But don't think that! (*On the point of tears.*) I couldn't
bear it! It'd be yust too much to know you was going away
where I'd never see you again – thinking that about me!

BURKE (*after an inward struggle – tensely – forcing out the words with
difficulty*). If I was believing – that you'd never had love for any

other man in the world but me – I could be forgetting the rest, maybe.

ANNA (*with a cry of joy*). Mat!

BURKE (*slowly*). If 'tis truth you're after telling, I'd have a right, maybe, to believe you'd changed – and that I'd changed you myself till the thing you'd been all your life wouldn't be you any more at all.

ANNA (*hanging on his words – breathlessly*). Oh, Mat! That's what I been trying to tell you all along!

BURKE (*simply*). For I've got a power of strength in me to lead men the way I want, and women, too, maybe, and I'm thinking I'd change you to a new woman entirely, so I'd never know, or you either, what kind of woman you'd been in the past at all.

ANNA. Yes, you could, Mat! I know you could!

BURKE. And I'm thinking 'twasn't your fault, maybe, but having that old ape for a father that left you to grow up alone, made you what you was. And if I could be believing 'tis only me you –

ANNA (*distractedly*). You got to believe it, Mat! What can I do? I'll do anything, anything you want to prove I'm not lying!

BURKE (*suddenly seems to have a solution. He feels in the pocket of his coat and grasps something – solemnly*). Would you be willing to swear an oath, now – a terrible, fearful oath would send your soul to the divils in hell if you was lying?

ANNA (*eagerly*). Sure, I'll swear, Mat – on anything!

BURKE (*takes a small, cheap old crucifix from his pocket and holds it up for her to see*). Will you swear on this?

ANNA (*reaching out for it*). Yes. Sure I will. Give it to me.

BURKE (*holding it away*). 'Tis a cross was given me by my mother, God rest her soul. (*He makes the sign of the cross mechanically.*) I was a lad only, and she told me to keep it by me if I'd be waking or sleeping and never lose it, and it'd bring me luck. She died soon after. But I'm after keeping it with me from that day to this, and I'm telling you there's great power in it, and 'tis great bad luck it's saved me from and me roaming the seas, and I having it tied round my neck when my last ship sunk, and it bringing me safe to land when the others went to their death. (*Very earnestly.*) And I'm warning you now, if you'd swear

an oath on this, 'tis my old woman herself will be looking down
from Hivin above, and praying Almighty God and the Saints to
put a great curse on you if she'd hear you swearing a lie!

ANNA (*awed by his manner – superstitiously*). I wouldn't have the
nerve – honest – if it was a lie. But it's the truth and I ain't
scared to swear. Give it to me.

BURKE (*handing it to her – almost frightened, as if he feared for her
safety*). Be careful what you'd swear, I'm saying.

ANNA (*holding the cross gingerly*). Well – what do you want me to
swear? You say it.

BURKE. Swear I'm the only man in the world ivir you felt love
for.

ANNA (*looking into his eyes steadily*). I swear it.

BURKE. And that you'll be forgetting from this day all the
badness you've done and never do the like of it again.

ANNA (*forcibly*). I swear it! I swear it by God!

BURKE. And may the blackest curse of God strike you if you're
lying. Say it now!

ANNA. And may the blackest curse of God strike me if I'm lying!

BURKE (*with a stupendous sigh*). Oh, glory be to God, I'm after
believing you now! (*He takes the cross from her hand, his face
beaming with joy, and puts it back in his pocket. He puts his arm about
her waist and is about to kiss her when he stops, appalled by some
terrible doubt.*)

ANNA (*alarmed*). What's the matter with you?

BURKE (*with sudden fierce questioning*). Is it Catholic ye are?

ANNA (*confused*). No. Why?

BURKE (*filled with a sort of bewildered foreboding*). Oh, God, help
me! (*With a dark glance of suspicion at her.*) There's some divil's
trickery in it, to be swearing an oath on a Catholic cross and
you wan of the others.

ANNA (*distractedly*). Oh, Mat, don't you believe me?

BURKE (*miserably*). If it isn't a Catholic you are –

ANNA. I ain't nothing. What's the difference? Didn't you hear
me swear?

BURKE (*passionately*). Oh, I'd a right to stay away from you – but I couldn't! I was loving you in spite of it all, and wanting to be with you, God forgive me, no matter what you are. I'd go mad if I'd not have you! I'd be killing the world -- (*He seizes her in his arms and kisses her fiercely.*)

ANNA (*with a gasp of joy*). Mat!

BURKE (*suddenly holding her away from him and staring into her eyes as if to probe into her soul – slowly*). If your oath is no proper oath at all, I'll have to be taking your naked word for it and have you anyway, I'm thinking – I'm needing you that bad!

ANNA (*hurt – reproachfully*). Mat! I swore, didn't I?

BURKE (*defiantly, as if challenging fate*). Oath or no oath, 'tis no matter. We'll be wedded in the morning, with the help of God. (*Still more defiantly.*) We'll be happy now, the two of us, in spite of the divil!

He crushes her to him and kisses her again. The door on the left is pushed open and CHRIS appears in the doorway. He stands blinking at them. At first the old expression of hatred of BURKE comes into his eyes instinctively. Then a look of resignation and relief takes its place. His face lights up with a sudden happy thought. He turns back into the bedroom – reappears immediately with the tin can of beer in his hand – grinning.

CHRIS. Ve have a drink on this, py golly! (*They break away from each other with startled exclamations.*)

BURKE (*explosively*). God stiffen it! (*He takes a step toward CHRIS threateningly.*)

ANNA (*happily – to her father*). That's the way to talk! (*With a laugh.*) And say, it's about time for you and Mat to kiss and make up. You're going to be shipmates on the *Londonderry*, did you know it?

BURKE (*astounded*). Shipmates – Has himself –

CHRIS (*equally astounded*). Ay vas bos'n on her.

BURKE. The divil! (*Then angrily.*) You'd be going back to sea and leaving her alone, would you?

ANNA (*quickly*). It's all right, Mat. That's where he belongs, and I want him to go. You got to go, too; we'll need the money. (*With a laugh, as she gets the glasses.*) And as for me being alone, that runs in the family, and I'll get used to it. (*Pouring out their glasses.*) I'll get a little house somewhere, and I'll make a regular place for you two to come back to – wait and see. And now you drink up and be friends.

BURKE (*happily – but still a bit resentful against the old man*). Sure! (*Clinking his glass against* CHRIS'*s.*) Here's luck to you! (*He drinks.*)

CHRIS (*subdued – his face melancholy*). Skoal. (*He drinks.*)

BURKE (*to* ANNA, *with a wink*). You'll not be lonesome long. I'll see to that, with the help of God. 'Tis himself here will be having a grandchild to ride on his foot, I'm telling you!

ANNA (*turning away in embarrassment*). Quit the kidding, now.

She picks up her bag and goes into the room on left. As soon as she is gone BURKE *relapses into an attitude of gloomy thought.* CHRIS *stares at his beer absentmindedly. Finally* BURKE *turns on him.*

BURKE. Is it any religion at all you have, you and your Anna?

CHRIS (*surpised*). Vhy yes, Ve vas Lutheran in ole country.

BURKE (*horrified*). Luthers, is it? (*Then with a grim resignation, slowly, aloud to himself*). Well, I'm damned then surely. Yerra, what's the difference? 'Tis the will of God, anyway.

CHRIS (*moodily preoccupied with his own thoughts – speaks with sombre premonition as* ANNA *re-enters from the left.*) It's funny. It's queer, yes – you and me shipping on same boat dat vay. It ain't right. Ay don't know – it's dat funny vay ole davil sea do her vorst dirty tricks, yes. It's so. (*He gets up and goes back, and opening the door, stares out into the darkness.*)

BURKE (*nodding his head in gloomy acquiescence – with a great sigh*). I'm fearing maybe you have the right of it for once, divil take you.

ANNA (*forcing a laugh*). Gee, Mat, you ain't agreeing with him, are you? (*She comes forward and puts her arm about his shoulder – with a determined gaiety.*) Aw say, what's the matter? Cut out the gloom. We're all fixed now, ain't we, me and you? (*Pours out more beer into his glass and fills one for herself – slaps him on the back.*) Come on! Here's to the sea, no matter what! Be a game sport and drink to that! Come on! (*She gulps down her glass.* BURKE *banishes his superstitious premonitions with a defiant jerk of his head, grins up at her, and drinks to her toast.*)

CHRIS (*looking out into the night – lost in his sombre preoccupation – shakes his head and mutters*). Fog, fog, fog, all bloody time. You can't see vhere you vas going, no. Only dat ole davil, sea – she knows! (*The two stare at him. From the harbour comes the muffled, mournful wail of steamers' whistles.*)

The curtain falls.

THE EMPEROR JONES

Characters

BRUTUS JONES, Emperor
HENRY SMITHERS, A Cockney Trader
AN OLD NATIVE WOMAN
LEM, A Native Chief
SOLDIERS, Adherents of Lem
The Little Formless Fears; Jeff; the Negro Convicts; the Prison
Guard; the Planters; the Auctioneer; the Slaves; the Congo
Witch-Doctor; the Crocodile God

The action of the play takes place on an island in the West Indies
as yet not self-determined by White Mariners. The form of native
government is, for the time being, an Empire.

Scene One

The audience chamber in the palace of the Emperor – a spacious, high-ceilinged room with bare, whitewashed walls. The floor is of white tiles. In the rear, to the left of centre, a wide archway giving out on a portico with white pillars. The palace is evidently situated on high ground, for beyond the portico nothing can be seen but a vista of distant hills, their summits crowned with thick groves of palm trees. In the right wall, centre, a smaller arched doorway leading to the living quarters of the palace. The room is bare of furniture with the exception of one huge chair made of uncut wood which stands at centre, its back to rear. This is very apparently the Emperor's throne. It is painted a dazzling, eye-smiting scarlet. There is a brilliant orange cushion on the seat and another smaller one is placed on the floor to serve as a footstool. Strips of matting, dyed scarlet, lead from the foot of the throne to the two entrances.

It is late afternoon, but the yellow sunlight still blazes beyond the portico and there is an oppressive burden of exhausting heat in the air.

As the curtain rises, a native NEGRO WOMAN *sneaks in cautiously from the entrance on the right. She is very old, dressed in cheap calico, bare-footed, a red bandana handkerchief covering all but a few stray wisps of white hair. A bundle bound in coloured cloth is carried over her shoulder on the end of a stick. She hesitates beside the doorway, peering back as if in extreme dread of being discovered. Then she begins to glide noiselessly, a step at a time, towards the doorway in the rear. At this moment* SMITHERS *appears beneath the portico.*

SMITHERS *is a tall man, round-shouldered, about forty. His bald head, perched on a long neck with an enormous Adam's apple, looks like an egg. The tropics have tanned his naturally pasty face with its small, sharp features to a sickly yellow, and native rum has painted his pointed nose to a startling red. His little washy-blue eyes are red-rimmed and dart about him like a ferret's. His expression is one of unscrupulous meanness, cowardly and dangerous. He is dressed in a worn riding suit of dirty white drill, puttees, and spurs, and wears a white cork helmet. A cartridge belt with an automatic revolver is around his waist. He carries a riding whip in his hand. He sees the woman and stops to watch her suspiciously. Then, making up his mind, he steps quickly on tiptoe into the room. The* WOMAN, *looking back over her shoulder continually, does not see him until it is too late. When she does* SMITHERS *springs forward and grabs her firmly by the shoulder. She struggles to get away, fiercely but silently.*

SMITHERS (*tightening his grasp – roughly*). Easy! None o' that, me birdie. You can't wriggle out now. I got me 'ooks on yer.

WOMAN (*seeing the uselessness of struggling, gives way to frantic terror, and sinks to the ground, embracing his knees supplicatingly*). No tell him! No tell him, Mister!

SMITHERS (*with great curiosity*). Tell 'im? (*Then scornfully.*) Oh, you mean 'is bloomin' Majesty. What's the game, any 'ow? What are you sneakin' away for? Been stealin' a bit, I s'pose. (*He taps her bundle with his riding whip significantly.*)

WOMAN (*shaking her head vehemently*). No, me no steal.

SMITHERS. Bloody liar! But tell me what's up. There's somethin' funny goin' on. I smelled it in the air first thing I got up this mornin'. You blacks are up to some devilment. This palace of 'is is like a bleedin' tomb. Where's all the 'ands? (*The* WOMAN *keeps sullenly silent.* SMITHERS *raises his whip threateningly.*) Ow, yer won't, won't yer? I'll show yer what's what.

WOMAN (*coweringly*). I tell, Mister. You no hit. They go – all go. (*She makes a sweeping gesture towards the hills in the distance.*)

SMITHERS. Run away – to the 'ills?

WOMAN. Yes, Mister. Him Emperor – Great Father. (*She touches her forehead to the floor with a quick mechanical jerk.*) Him sleep after eat. Then they go – all go. Me old woman. Me left only. Now me go too.

SMITHERS (*his astonishment giving way to an immense, mean satisfaction*). Ow! So that's the ticket! Well, I know bloody well wot's in the air – when they runs orf to the 'ills. The tom-tom'll be thumping out there bloomin' soon. (*With extreme vindictiveness.*) And I'm bloody glad of it, for one! Serve 'im right! Puttin' on airs, the stinkin' nigger! 'Is Majesty! Gawd blimey! I only 'opes I'm there when they takes 'im out to shoot 'im. (*Suddenly.*) 'E's still 'ere all right, ain't 'e?

WOMAN. Yes. Him sleep.

SMITHERS. 'E's bound to find out soon as 'e wakes up. 'E's cunnin' enough to know when 'is time's come. (*He goes to the doorway on right and whistles shrilly with his fingers in his mouth. The* OLD WOMAN *springs to her feet and runs out of the doorway, rear.*

SMITHERS *goes after her, reaching for his revolver.*) Stop or I'll shoot! (*Then stopping – indifferently.*) Pop orf then, if yer like, yer black cow. (*He stands in the doorway, looking after her.*)

JONES *enters from the right. He is a tall, powerfully built, full-blooded Negro of middle age. His features are typically negroid, yet there is something decidedly distinctive about his face – an underlying strength of will, a hardy, self-reliant confidence in himself that inspires respect. His eyes are alive with a keen, cunning intelligence. In manner he is shrewd, suspicious, evasive. He wears a light blue uniform coat, sprayed with brass buttons, heavy gold chevrons on his shoulders, gold braid on the collar, cuffs, etc. His trousers are bright red with a light blue stripe down the side. Patent-leather laced boots with brass spurs, and a belt with a long-barrelled, pearl-handled revolver in a holster complete his attire. Yet there is something not altogether ridiculous about his grandeur. He has a way of carrying it off.*

JONES (*not seeing anyone – greatly irritated and blinking sleepily – shouts*). Who dare whistle dat way in my palace? Who dare wake up de Emperor? I'll git de hide flayed off some o' you niggers sho'!

SMITHERS (*showing himself – in a manner half-afraid and half-defiant*). It was me whistled to yer. (*As* JONES *frowns angrily.*) I got news for yer.

JONES (*putting on his suavest manner, which fails to cover up his contempt for the white man*). Oh, it's you, Mister Smithers. (*He sits down on his throne with easy dignity.*) What news you got to tell me?

SMITHERS (*coming close to enjoy his discomfiture*). Don't yer notice nothin' funny today?

JONES (*coldly*). Funny? No. I ain't perceived nothin' of de kind!

SMITHERS. Then yer ain't so foxy as I thought yer was. Where's all your court? (*Sarcastically.*) The Generals and the Cabinet Ministers and all?

JONES (*imperturbably*). Where dey mostly runs to minute I closes my eyes – drinkin' rum and talkin' big down in de town. (*Sarcastically.*) How come you don't know dat? Ain't you carousing with 'em most every day?

SMITHERS (*stung, but pretending indifference – with a wink*). That's part of the day's work. I got ter – ain't I – in my business?

JONES (*contemptuously*). Yo' business!

SMITHERS (*imprudently enraged*). Gawd blimey, you was glad
enough for me ter take yer in on it when you landed 'ere first.
You didn't 'ave no 'igh and mighty airs in them days!

JONES (*his hand going to his revolver like a flash – menacingly*). Talk
polite, white man! Talk polite, you heah me! I'm boss heah
now, is you fergettin'?

*The Cockney seems about to challenge this last statement with the facts,
but something in the other's eyes holds and cows him.*

SMITHERS (*in a cowardly whine*). No 'arm meant, old top.

JONES (*condescendingly*). I accepts yo' apology. (*Lets his hand fall
from his revolver.*) No use'n you rakin' up ole times. What I was
den is one thing. What I is now's another. You didn't let me in
on yo' crooked work out o' no kind feelin's dat time. I done de
dirty work fo' you – and most o' de brain work, too, fo' dat
matter – and I was wu'th money to you, dat's de reason.

SMITHERS. Well, blimey, I give yer a start, didn't I – when no
one else would. I wasn't afraid to 'ire yer like the rest was –
'count of the story about your breakin' jail back in the States.

JONES. No, you didn't have no s'cuse to look down on me fo'
dat. You been in jail you'self more'n once.

SMITHERS (*furiously*). It's a lie! (*Then trying to pass it off by an
attempt at scorn.*) Garn! Who told yer that fairy tale?

JONES. Dey's some tings I ain't got to be tole. I kin see 'em in
folk's eyes. (*Then after a pause – meditatively.*) Yes, you sho' give
me a start. And it didn't take long from dat time to git dese
fool woods' niggers right where I wanted dem. (*With pride.*)
From stowaway to Emperor in two years! Dat's goin' some!

SMITHERS (*with curiosity*). And I bet you got yer pile o'money 'id
safe some place.

JONES (*with satisfaction*). I sho' has! And it's in a foreign bank
where no pusson don't ever git it out but me no matter what
come. You didn't s'pose I was holdin' down dis Emperor job
for de glory in it, did you? Sho'! De fuss and glory part of it,
dat's only to turn de heads o' de low-flung bush niggers dat's
here. Dey wants de big circus show for deir money. I gives it to
'em an' I gits de money. (*With a grin.*) De long green, dat's me
every time! (*Then rebukingly.*) But you ain't got no kick agin me,
Smithers. I'se paid you back all you done for me many times.
Ain't I pertected you and winked at all de crooked tradin' you

been doin' right out in de broad day. Sho' I has – and me makin' laws to stop it at de same time! (*He chuckles.*)

SMITHERS (*grinning*). But, meanin' no 'arm, you been grabbin' right and left yourself, ain't yer! Look at the taxes you've put on 'em! Blimey! You've squeezed 'em dry!

JONES (*chuckling*). No, dey ain't *all* dry yet. I'se still heah, ain't I?

SMITHERS (*smiling at his secret thought*). They're dry right now, you'll find out. (*Changing the subject abruptly.*) And as for me breakin' laws, you've broke 'em all yerself just as fast as yer made 'em.

JONES. Ain't I de Emperor? De laws don't go for him. (*Judicially.*) You heah what I tells you, Smithers. Dere's little stealin' like you does, and dere's big stealin' like I does. For de little stealin' dey gits you in jail soon or late. For de big stealin' dey makes you Emperor and puts you in de Hall o' Fame when you croaks. (*Reminiscently.*) If dey's one thing I learns in ten years on de Pullman ca's listenin' to de white quality talk, it's dat same fact. And when I gits a chance to use it I winds up Emperor in two years.

SMITHERS (*unable to repress the genuine admiration of the small fry for the large*). Yes, yer turned the bleedin' trick, all right. Blimey, I never seen a bloke 'as 'ad the bloomin' luck you 'as.

JONES (*severely*). Luck? What you mean – luck?

SMITHERS. I suppose you'll say as that swank about the silver bullet ain't luck – and that was what first got the fool blacks on yer side the time of the revolution, wasn't it?

JONES (*with a laugh*). Oh, dat silver bullet! Sho' was luck! But I makes dat luck, you heah? I loads de dice! Yessuh! When dat murderin' nigger ole Lem hired to kill me takes aim ten feet away and his gun misses fire and I shoots him dead, what you heah me say?

SMITHERS. You said yer'd got a charm so's no lead bullet'd kill yer. You was so strong only a silver bullet could kill yer, you told 'em. Blimey, wasn't that swank for yer, and plain, fat-'eaded luck?

JONES (*proudly*). I got brains and I uses 'em quick. Dat ain't luck.

SMITHERS. Yer know they wasn't 'ardly liable to get no silver bullets. And it was luck 'e didn't 'it you that time.

JONES (*laughing*). And dere all dem fool bush niggers was kneelin' down and bumpin' deir heads on de ground like I was a miracle out o' de Bible. Oh Lawd, from dat time on I has dem all eatin' out of my hand. I cracks de whip and dey jumps through.

SMITHERS (*with a sniff*). Yankee bluff done it.

JONES. Ain't a man's talkin' big what makes him big – long as he makes folks believe it? Sho', I talks large when I ain't got nothin' to back it up, but I ain't talkin' wild just de same. I knows I kin fool 'em – I *knows* it – and dat's backin' enough fo' my game. And ain't I got to learn deir lingo and teach some of dem English befo' I kin talk to em? Ain't dat wuk? You ain't never learned any word of it, Smithers, in de ten years you been heah, dough you knows it's money in yo' pocket tradin' wid 'em if you does. But you'se too shiftless to take de trouble.

SMITHERS (*flushing*). Never mind about me. What's this I've 'eard about yer really 'avin' a silver bullet moulded for yourself?'

JONES. It's playin' out my bluff. I has de silver bullet moulded and I tells 'em when de time comes I kills myself wid it. I tells 'em dat's 'cause I'm de on'y man in de world big enuff to git me. No use'n deir tryin'. And dey falls down and bumps deir heads. (*He laughs.*) I does dat so's I kin take a walk in peace widout no jealous nigger gunnin' at me from behind de trees.

SMITHERS (*astonished*). Then you 'ad it made – 'onest?

JONES. Sho' did. Heah she be. (*He takes out his revolver, breaks it, and takes the bullet out of one chamber.*) Five lead an' dis silver baby at de last. Don't she shine pretty? (*He holds it in his hand, looking at it admiringly, as if strangely fascinated.*)

SMITHERS. Let me see. (*Reaches out his hand for it.*)

JONES (*harshly*). Keep yo' hands whar dey b'long, white man. (*He replaces it in the chamber and puts the revolver back on his hip.*)

SMITHERS (*snarling*). Gawd blimey! Think I'm a bleedin' thief, you would.

JONES. No, 'tain't dat. I knows you'se scared to steal from me. On'y I ain't 'lowin' nary body to touch dis baby. She's my rabbit's foot.

SMITHERS (*sneering*). A bloomin' charm, wot? (*Venomously.*) Well, you'll need all the bloody charms you 'as before long, s' 'elp me!

JONES (*judicially*). Oh, I'se good for six months yit 'fore dey gits sick o' my game. Den, when I sees trouble comin', I makes a move.

SMITHERS. Ho! You got it all planned, ain't yer?

JONES. I ain't no fool. I know dis Emperor's time is sho't. Dat why I make hay when de sun shine. Was you thinkin' I'se aimin' to hold down dis job for life? No, suh! What good is gittin' money if you stays back in dis raggedy country? I wants action when I spends. And when I sees dese niggers gittin' up deir nerve to tu'n me out, and I'se got all de money in sight, I resigns on de spot and gets away quick.

SMITHERS. Where to?

JONES. None o' yo' business.

SMITHERS. Not back to the bloody States, I'll lay my oath.

JONES (*suspiciously*). Why don't I? (*Then with an easy laugh.*) You mean 'count of dat story 'bout me breakin' from jail back dere? Dat's all talk.

SMITHERS (*sceptically*). Ho, yes!

JONES (*sharply*). You ain't 'sinuatin' I'se a liar, is you?

SMITHERS (*hastily*). No, Gawd strike me! I was only thinkin' o' the bloody lies you told the blacks 'ere about killin' white men in the States.

JONES (*angered*). How come dey're lies?

SMITHERS. You'd 'ave been in jail if you 'ad, wouldn't yer then? (*With venom.*) And from what I've 'eard, it ain't 'ealthy for a black to kill a white man in the States. They burns 'em in oil, don't they?

JONES (*with cool deadliness*). You mean lynchin' 'd scare me? Well, I tells you, Smithers, maybe I does kill one white man back dere. Maybe I does. And maybe I kills another right heah 'fore long if he don't look out.

SMITHERS (*trying to force a laugh*). I was on'y spoofin' yer. Can't yer take a joke? And you was just sayin' you'd never been in jail.

JONES (*in the same tone – slightly boastful*). Maybe I goes to jail dere for gettin' in an argument wid razors ovah a game of dice. Maybe I gits twenty years when dat coloured man die. Maybe I gits in 'nother argument wid de prison guard and de overseer ovah us when we're wukin' de roads. Maybe he hits me wid a whip and I splits his head wid a shovel and runs away and files de chain off my leg and gits away safe. Maybe I does all dat an' maybe I don't. It's a story I tells you so's you knows I'se de kind of man dat if you evah repeats one word of it, I ends yo' stealin' on dis yearth mighty damn quick!

SMITHERS (*terrified*). Think I'd peach on yer? Not me! Ain't I always been yer friend?

JONES (*suddenly relaxing*). Sho' you has – and you better be.

SMITHERS (*recovering his composure – and with it his malice*). And just to show yer I'm yer friend, I'll tell you that bit o' news I was goin' to.

JONES. Go ahead! Must be bad news from de happy way you look.

SMITHERS (*warningly*). Maybe it's gettin' time for you to resign – with that bloomin' silver bullet, wot? (*He finishes with a mocking grin.*)

JONES (*puzzled*). What's dat you say? Talk plain.

SMITHERS. Ain't noticed any of the guards or servants about the place today, I 'aven't.

JONES (*carelessly*). Dey're all out in de garden sleepin' under de trees. When I sleeps, dey sneaks a sleep too, and I pretends I never suspicions it. All I got to do is to ring de bell and dey come flyin', makin' a bluff dey was wukin' all de time.

SMITHERS (*in the same mocking tone*). Ring the bell now an' you'll bloody well see what I mean.

JONES (*startled to alertness, but preserving the same careless tone*). Sho' I rings.

He reaches below the throne and pulls out a big common dinner bell which is painted the same vivid scarlet as the throne. He rings this vigorously – then stops to listen. Then he goes to both doors, rings again, and looks out.

SMITHERS (*watching him with malicious satisfaction, after a pause – mockingly*). The bloody ship is sinkin' an' the bleedin' rats 'as slung their 'ooks.

JONES (*in a sudden fit of anger flings the bell clattering into a corner*). Low-flung bush niggers! (*Then catching SMITHERS' eye on him,*

he controls himself and suddenly bursts into a low chuckling laugh.)
Reckon I overplays my hand dis once! A man can't take de pot
on a short-tailed flush all de time. Was I sayin' I'd sit six
months mo'? Well, I'se changed my mind den. I gives in and
resigns de job of Emperor right dis minute.

SMITHERS (*with real admiration*). Blimey, but you're a cool bird,
and no mistake.

JONES. No use'n fussin'. When I knows de game's up I kisses it
good-bye widout no long waits. Dey've all run off to de hills,
ain't dey?

SMITHERS. Yes – every bleedin' man jack of 'em.

JONES. Den de revolution is at de door. And de Emperor better
git his feet movin' up de trail. (*He starts for the door in rear.*)

SMITHERS. Goin' out to look for your 'orse? Yer won't find any.
They steals the 'orses first thing. Mine was gone when I went
for 'im this mornin'. That's wot first give me a suspicion of wot
was up.

JONES (*alarmed for a second, scratches his head, then philosophically*).
Well, den I hoofs it. Feet, do yo' duty! (*He pulls out a gold watch
and looks at it.*) Three-thuty. Sundown's at six-thuty or
dereabouts. (*Puts his watch back – with cool confidence.*) I got
plenty o' time to make it easy.

SMITHERS. Don't be so bloomin' sure of it. They'll be after you
'ot and 'eavy. Ole Lem is at the bottom o' this business an' 'e
'ates you like 'ell. 'E'd rather do for you than eat 'is dinner, 'e
would!

JONES (*scornfully*). Dat fool no-count nigger! Does you think I'se
scared o' him? I stands him on his thick head more'n once befo'
dis, and I does it again if he comes in my way – (*Fiercely.*) And
dis time I leave him a dead nigger fo' sho'!

SMITHERS. You'll 'ave to cut through the big forest – an' these
blacks 'ere can sniff and follow a trail in the dark like 'ounds.
You'd 'ave to 'ustle to get through that forest in twelve hours
even if you knew all the bloomin' paths like a native.

JONES (*with indignant scorn*). Look-a-heah, white man! Does you
think I'se a natural bo'n fool? Give me credit fo' havin' some
sense, fo' Lawd's sake! Don't you s'pose I'se looked ahead and
made sho' of all de chances? I'se gone out in dat big forest,
pretendin' to hunt, so many times dat I knows it high an' low
like a book. I could go through on dem paths wid my eyes

shut. (*With great contempt.*) Think dese ig'nerent bush niggers
dat ain't got brains enuff to know deir own names even, can
catch Brutus Jones? Huh, I s'pects not! Not on yo' life! Why,
man, de white men went after me wid bloodhounds, where I
come from an' I jes' laughs at 'em. It's a shame to fool dese
black trash around heah, dey're so easy. You watch me, man.
I'll make dem look sick, I will. I'll be 'cross de plain to de edge
of de forest by time dark comes. Once in de woods in de night,
dey got a fine chance o' findin' dis baby! Dawn tomorrow I'll be
out at de oder side and on de coast whar dat French gunboat is
stayin'. She picks me up, take me to the Martinique when she
go dar, and dere I safe wid a mighty big bankroll in my pocket.
It's easy as rollin' off a log.

SMITHERS (*maliciously*). But s'posin' somethin' 'appens wrong an'
they do nab yer?

JONES (*decisively*). Dey don't – dat's de answer.

SMITHERS. But, just for argyment's sake – what'd you do?

JONES (*frowning*). I'se got five lead bullets in dis gun good enuff
fo' common bush niggers – and after dat I got de silver bullet
to cheat 'em out o' gittin' me.

SMITHERS (*jeeringly*). Ho, I was fergettin' that silver bullet.
You'll bump yourself orf in style, won't yer? Blimey!

JONES (*gloomily*). You kin bet yo' whole money on one thing,
white man. Dis baby plays out his string to de end and when he
quits, he quits wid a bang de way he ought. Silver bullet ain't
none too good for him when he go, dat's a fac'! (*Then shaking
off his nervousness – with a confident laugh.*) Sho'! What is I talkin'
about? Ain't come to dat yit and I never will – not wid trash
niggers like dese yere. (*Boastfully.*) Silver bullet bring me luck
anyway. I kin outguess, outrun, outfight, an' outplay de whole
lot o' dem all ovah de board any time o' de day er night! You
watch me!

*From the distant hills comes the faint, steady thump of a tom-tom, low
and vibrating. It starts at a rate exactly corresponding to normal pulse
beat – seventy-two to the minute – and continues at a gradually
accelerating rate from this point uninterruptedly to the very end of the
play.*

JONES. (*Starts at the sound. A strange look of apprehension creeps into
his face for a moment as he listens. Then he asks, with an attempt to
regain his most casual manner*). What's dat drum beatin' fo'?

SMITHERS (*with a mean grin*). For you. That means the bleedin' ceremony 'as started. I've 'eard it before and I knows.

JONES. Cer'mony? What cer'mony?

SMITHERS. The blacks is 'oldin' a bloody meetin', 'avin' a war dance, gettin' their courage worked up b'fore they starts after you.

JONES. Let dem! Dey'll sho' need it!

SMITHERS. And they're there 'oldin' their 'eathen religious service – makin' no end of devil spells and charms to 'elp 'em against your silver bullet. (*He guffaws loudly.*) Blimey, but they're balmy as 'ell!

JONES (*a tiny bit awed and shaken in spite of himself*). Huh! Takes more'n dat to scare dis chicken!

SMITHERS (*scenting the other's feeling – maliciously*). Ternight when it's pitch black in the forest, they'll 'ave their pet devils and ghosts 'oundin' after you. You'll find yer bloody 'air 'll be standin' on end before termorrow mornin'. (*Seriously.*) It's a bleedin' queer place, that stinkin' forest, even in daylight. Yer don't know what might 'appen in there, it's that rotten still. Always sends the cold shivers down my back minute I gets in it.

JONES (*with a contemptuous sniff*). I ain't no white-liver like you is. Trees an' me, we'se friends, and dar's a full moon comin' bring me light. And let dem po' niggers make all de fool spells dey'se a min' to. Does yo' s'pect I'se silly enuff to b'lieve in ghosts an' ha'nts an' all dat ole woman's talk? G'long, white man! You ain't talkin' to me. (*With a chuckle.*) Doesn't you know dey's got to do wid a man who was member in good standin' o' de Baptist Church? Sho' I was dat when I was porter on de Pullmans, befo' I gits into my little trouble. Let dem try deir heathen tricks. De Baptist Church done pertect me and land dem all in hell. (*Then with more confident satisfaction.*) And I'se got little silver bullet o' my own, don't forgit.

SMITHERS. Ho! You 'aven't give much 'eed to your Baptist Church since you been down 'ere. I've 'eard myself you 'ad turned yer coat an' was takin' up with their blarsted witch-doctors, or whatever the 'ell yer calls the swine.

JONES (*vehemently*). I pretends to! Sho' I pretends! Dat's part o' my game from de fust. If I finds out dem niggers believes dat black is white, den I yells it out louder 'n deir loudest. It don't git me nothin' to do missionary work for de Baptist Church.

I'se after de coin, an' I lays my Jesus on de shelf for de time bein'. (*Stops abruptly to look at his watch – alertly.*) But I ain't got de time to waste no more fool talk wid you. I'se gwine away from heah dis secon'. (*He reaches in under the throne and pulls out an expensive Panama hat with a bright multi-coloured band and sets it jauntily on his head.*) So long, white man! (*With a grin.*) See you in jail some time, maybe!

SMITHERS. Not me, you won't. Well, I wouldn't be in yer bloody boots for no bloomin' money, but 'ere's wishin' yer luck just the same.

JONES (*contemptuously*). You're de frightenedest man evah I see! I tells you I'se safe's 'f I was in New York City. It takes dem niggers from now to dark to git up de nerve to start somethin'. By dat time, I'se got a head start dey never kotch up wid.

SMITHERS (*maliciously*). Give my regards to any ghosts yer meets up with.

JONES (*grinning*). If dat ghost got money, I'll tell him never ha'nt you less'n he wants to lose it.

SMITHERS (*flattered*). Garn! (*Then curiously.*) Ain't yer takin' no luggage with yer?

JONES. I travels light when I wants to move fast. And I got tinned grub buried on de edge o' de forest. (*Boastfully.*) Now say dat I don't look ahead an' use my brains! (*With a wide, liberal gesture.*) I will all dat's left in de palace to you – and you better grab all you kin sneak away wid befo' dey gits here.

SMITHERS (*gratefully*). Righto – and thanks ter yer. (*As* JONES *walks towards the door in rear – cautioningly.*) Say! Look 'ere, you ain't goin' out that way, are yer?

JONES. Does you think I'd slink out de back door like a common nigger? I'se Emperor yit, ain't I? And de Emperor Jones leaves de way he comes, and dat black trash don't dare stop him – not yit, leastways. (*He stops for a moment in the doorway, listening to the far-off but insistent beat of the tom-tom.*) Listen to dat roll-call, will you? Must be mighty big drum carry dat far. (*Then with a laugh.*) Well, if dey ain't no whole brass band to see me off, I sho' got de drum part of it. So long, white man.

He puts his hands in his pockets and with studied carelessness, whistling a tune, he saunters out of the doorway and off to left.

SMITHERS (*looks after him with a puzzled admiration*). 'E's got 'is
bloomin' nerve with 'im s'elp me! (*Then angrily.*) Ho – the
bleedin' nigger – puttin' on 'is bloody airs! I 'opes they nabs 'im
an' gives 'im what's what! (*Then putting business before the pleasure
of this thought, looking around him with cupidity.*) A bloke ought to
find a 'ole lot in this palace that'd go for a bit of cash. Let's take
a look, 'Arry, me lad.

He starts for the doorway on right as the curtain falls.

Scene Two

Nightfall

*The end of the plain where the Great Forest begins. The foreground is
sandy, level ground dotted by a few stones and clumps of stunted bushes
cowering close against the earth to escape the buffeting of the trade wind.
In the rear the forest is a wall of darkness dividing the world. Only when
the eye becomes accustomed to the gloom can the outlines of separate
trunks of the nearest trees be made out, enormous pillars of deeper
blackness. A sombre monotone of wind lost in the leaves moans in the air.
Yet this sound serves but to intensify the impression of the forest's
relentless immobility, to form a background throwing into relief its
brooding, implacable silence.*

JONES *enters from the left, walking rapidly. He stops as he nears the
edge of the forest, looks around him quickly, peering into the dark as if
searching for some familiar landmark. Then, apparently satisfied that he
is where he ought to be, he throws himself on the ground, dog-tired.*

Well, heah I is. In de nick o' time, too! Little mo' an' it'd be
blacker'n de ace of spades heah-abouts. (*He pulls a bandana
handkerchief from his hip pocket and mops off his perspiring face.*)
Sho'! Gimme air! I'se done up sho' 'nuff. Dat soft Emperor job
ain't no trainin' fo' a long dash ovah dat plain in de brilin' sun.
(*Then with a chuckle.*) Cheah up, nigger, de worst is yet to come.
(*He lifts his head and stares at the forest. His chuckle peters out
abruptly. In a tone of awe.*) My goodness, look at dem woods, will
you? Dat no-count Smithers said dey'd be black an' he sho'
called de turn. (*Turning away from them quickly and looking down
at his feet, he snatches at a chance to change the subject – solicitously.*)
Feet, you is holdin' up yo' end fine an' I sutinly hopes you ain't
blisterin'. It's time you git a rest. (*He takes off his shoes, his eyes
studiously avoiding the forest. He feels the soles of his feet gingerly.*)

You is still in de pink – on'y a little mite feverish. Cool yo'selfs. Remember you got a long journey yit before you. (*He sits in a weary attitude, listening to the rhythmic beating of the tom-tom. He grumbles in a loud tone to cover up a growing uneasiness.*) Bush niggers! Wonder dey wouldn' git sick o' beatin' dat drum. Sounds louder, seem like. I wonder if dey's startin' after me? (*He scrambles to his feet, looking back across the plain.*) Couldn't see dem now, nohow, if dey was hundred feet away. (*Then shaking himself like a wet dog to get rid of these depressing thoughts.*) Sho', dey's miles an' miles behind. What you gittin' fidgety about? (*But he sits down and begins to lace up his shoes in great haste, all the time muttering reassuringly.*) You know what? Yo' belly is empty, dat's what's de matter wid you. Come time to eat! Wid nothin' but wind on yo' stumach, o' course you feels jiggedy. Well, we eats right heah an' now soon's I gits dese here shoes laced up. (*He finishes lacing up his shoes.*) Dere! Now le's see! (*Gets on his hands and knees and searches the ground around him with his eyes.*) White stone, white stone, where is you? (*He sees the first white stone and crawls to it – with satisfaction.*) Heah you is! I knowed dis was de right place. Box of grub, come to me. (*He turns over the stone and feels in under it – in a tone of dismay.*) Ain't heah! Gorry, is I in de right place or isn't I? Dere's 'nother stone. Guess dat's it. (*He scrambles to the next stone and turns it over.*) Ain't heah, neither! Grub, whar is you? Ain't heah. Gorry, has I got to go hungry into dem woods – all de night? (*While he is talking he scrambles from one stone to another, turning them over in frantic haste. Finally he jumps to his feet excitedly.*) Is I lost de place? Must have! But how dat happen when I was followin' de trail across de plain in broad daylight? (*Almost plaintively.*) I'se hungry, I is! I gotta git my feed. Whar's my strength gonna come from if I doesn't? Gorry, I gotta find dat grub high an' low somehow! Why it come dark so quick like dat? Can't see nothin'. (*He scratches a match on his trousers and peers about him. The rate of the beat of the far-off tom-tom increases perceptibly as he does so. He mutters in a bewildered voice.*) How come all dese white stones come heah when I only remembers one? (*Suddenly, with a frightened gasp, he flings the match on the ground and stamps on it.*) Nigger, is you gone crazy mad? Is you lightin' matches to show dem whar you is? Fo' Lawd's sake, use yo' haid. Gorry, I'se got to be careful! (*He stares at the plain behind him apprehensively, his hand on his revolver.*) But how come all dese white stones? And whar's dat tin box o' grub I hid all wrapped up in oil cloth?

While his back is turned, the LITTLE FORMLESS FEARS *creep out from the deeper blackness of the forest. They are black, shapeless, only their glittering little eyes can be seen. If they have any describable form at all it is that of a grubworm about the size of a creeping child. They move noiselessly, but with deliberate, painful effort, striving to raise themselves on end, failing and sinking prone again. JONES turns about to face the forest. He stares up at the tops of the trees, seeking vainly to discover his whereabout by their conformation.*

Can't tell nothin' from dem trees! Gorry, nothin' 'round heah look like I evah seed it befo'. I'se gone lost de place sho' 'nuff. (*With mournful foreboding.*) It's mighty queer! It's mighty queer! (*With sudden forced defiance – in an angry tone.*) Woods, is you tryin' to put somethin' ovah on me? (*From the formless creatures on the ground in front of him comes a tiny gale of low mocking laughter like a rustling of leaves. They squirm upward towards him in twisted attitudes. JONES looks down, leaps backwards with a yell of terror, pulling out his revolver as he does so – in a quavering voice.*) What's dat? Who's dar? What is you? Git away from me befo' I shoots! You don't? –

He fires. There is a flash, a loud report, then silence broken only by the far-off quickened throb of the tom-tom. The formless creatures have scurried back into the forest. JONES remains fixed in his position listening intently. The sound of the shot, the reassuring feel of the revolver in his hand, have somewhat restored his shaken nerve. He addresses himself with renewed confidence.

Dey're gone. Dat shot fix 'em. Dey was only little animals – little wild pigs, I reckon. Dey've maybe rooted out yo' grub an' eat it. Sho', you fool nigger, what you think dey is – ha'nts. (*Excitedly.*) Gorry, you give de game away when you fire dat shot. Dem niggers heah dat fo' su'tin! Time you beat it in de woods widout no long waits.

He starts for the forest – hesitates before the plunge – then urging himself in with manful resolution.) Git in, nigger! What you skeered at? Ain't nothin' dere but de trees! Git in! (*He plunges boldly into the forest.*)

Scene Three

Nine o'clock. In the forest. The moon has just risen. Its beams, drifting through the canopy of leaves, make a barely perceptible, suffused, eerie glow. A dense low wall of underbrush and creepers is in the nearer forground, fencing in a small triangular clearing. Beyond this is the massed blackness of the forest like an encompassing barrier. A path is dimly discerned leading down to the clearing from left, rear, and winding away from it again towards the right.

As the scene opens nothing can be distinctly made out. Except for the beating of the tom-tom, which is a trifle louder and quicker than in the previous scene, there is silence, broken every few seconds by a queer, clicking sound. Then gradually the figure of the Negro, JEFF, can be discerned crouching on his haunches at the rear of the triangle. He is middle-aged, thin, brown in colour, is dressed in a Pullman porter's uniform, cap, etc. He is throwing a pair of dice on the ground before him, picking them up, shaking them, casting them out with the regular, rigid, mechanical movements of an automaton. The heavy, plodding footsteps of someone approaching along the trail from the left are heard and JONES's voice, pitched in a slightly higher key and strained in a cheering effort to overcome its own tremors.

JONES. De moon's rizen. Does you heah dat nigger? You gits more light from dis forrard. No mo' buttin' yo' fool head agin' de trunks an' scratchin' de hide off yo' legs in de bushes. Now you sees whar you'se gwine. So cheer up! From now on you has it easy. (*He steps just to the rear of the triangular clearing and mops off his face on his sleeve. He has lost his Panama hat. His face is scratched, his brilliant uniform shows several large rents.*) What time's it gittin' to be, I wonder? I dassent light no match to find out. Phoo'. It's wa'm an' dat's a fac! (*Wearily.*) How long I been makin' trampin' dese woods? Must be hours an' hours. Seems like fo'evah! Yit can't be, when de moon's jes riz. Dis am a long night fo' yo', yo' Majesty! (*With a mournful chuckle.*) Majesty! Der ain't much majesty 'bout dis baby now. (*With attempted cheerfulness.*) Never min'. It's all part o' de game. Dis night come to an end like everything else. And when you gits dar safe and has dat bankroll in yo' hands you laughs at all dis. (*He starts to whistle, but checks himself abruptly.*) What yo' whistlin' for, you po' fool! Want all de worl' to heah you? (*He stops talking to listen.*) Heah dat ole drum! Sho' gits nearer from de sound. Dey're takin' it along wid 'em. Time fo' me to move. (*He takes a step forward, then stops – worriedly.*) What's dat odder queer clickety sound I heah? Dere it is! Sound close! Sound like – sound like – Fo' God sake, sound like some nigger was shootin' dice! (*Frightenedly.*) I better get on quick when I gits dem notions. (*He walks quickly into the clear space – then stands transfixed as he sees JEFF – in a terrified gasp.*) Who dar? Who dat? Is dat you, Jeff? (*Starting towards the other, forgetful for a moment of his surroundings and really believing it is a living man that he sees – in a tone of happy relief.*) Jeff! I'se sho' mighty glad to see you! Dey tol' me you done died from dat razor cut I give you. (*Stopping suddenly, bewildered.*) But how you come to be heah, nigger? (*He stares fascinatedly at the other who continues his mechanical play with the dice. JONES's eyes begin to roll wildly. He stutters.*) Ain't you gwine – look up – can't you speak to me? Is you – is you – a ha'nt? (*He jerks out his revolver in a frenzy of terrified rage.*) Nigger, I kills you dead once. Has I got to kill you agin? You take it den. (*He fires. When the smoke clears away JEFF has disappeared. JONES stands trembling – then with a certain reassurance.*) He's gone, anyway. Ha'nt or no ha'nt, dat shot fix him. (*The beat of the far-off tom-tom is perceptibly louder and more rapid. JONES becomes conscious of it – with a start, looking back over his shoulder.*) Dey's gittin' near! Dey'se comin' fast! And heah I is shootin' shots to let 'em know jes' whar I is. Oh, Gorry, I'se got to run. (*Forgetting the path he plunges wildly into the underbrush in the rear and disappears in the shadow.*)

Scene Four

Eleven o'clock. In the forest. A wide dirt road runs diagonally from right, front, to left, rear. Rising sheer on both sides the forest walls it in. The moon is now up. Under its light the road glimmers ghastly and unreal. It is as if the forest has stood aside momentarily to let the road pass through and accomplish its veiled purpose. This done, the forest will fold in upon itself again and the road will be no more.

JONES stumbles in from the forest on the right. His uniform is ragged and torn. He looks about him with numbed surprise when he sees the road, his eyes blinking in the bright moonlight. He flops down exhaustedly and pants heavily for a while. Then with sudden anger.

JONES. I'm meltin' wid heat! Runnin' an' runnin' an' runnin'! Damn dis heah coat! Like a straight-jacket! (*He tears off his coat and flings it away from him, revealing himself stripped to the waist.*) Dere! Dat's better! Now I kin breathe! (*Looking down at his feet, the spurs catch his eye.*) And to hell wid dese high-fangled spurs. Dey're what's been a-trippin' me up an' breakin' me neck. (*He unstraps them and flings them away disgustedly.*) Dere! I gits rid o' dem frippety Emperor trappin's an' I travels lighter. Lawd! I'se tired! (*After a pause, listening to the insistent beat of the tom-tom in the distance.*) I must 'a put some distance between myself an'

dem – runnin' like dat – and yit – dat damn drum sound jes'
de same – nearer, even. Well, I guess I a'most holds my lead
anyhow. Dey won't never catch up. (*With a sigh.*) If on'y my fool
legs stands up. Oh, I'se sorry I evah went in for dis. Dat
Emperor job is sho' hard to shake. (*He looks around him
suspiciously.*) How'd dis road evah git heah? Good level road,
too. I never remembers seein' it befo'. (*Shaking his head
apprehensively.*) Dese woods is sho' full o' de queerest things at
night. (*With a sudden terror.*) Lawd God, don't let me see no
more o' dem ha'nts! Dey gits me scared! (*Then trying to talk
himself into confidence.*) Ha'nts! You fool nigger, dey ain't no
such things! Don't de Baptist parson tell you dat many time? Is
you civilized, or is you like dese ign'rent black niggers heah?
Sho'! Dat was all in yo' own head. Wasn't nothin' dere. Wasn't
no Jeff! Know what? You jus' get seein' dem things 'cause yo'
belly's empty and you's sick wid hunger inside. Hunger 'fects
yo' head and yo' eyes. Any fool know dat. (*Then pleading
fervently.*) But bless God, I don't come across no more o' dem,
whatever dey is! (*Then cautiously.*) Rest! Don't talk! Rest! You
needs it. Den you gits on yo' way again. (*Looking at the moon.*)
Night's half gone a'most. You hits de coast in de mawning! Den
you'se all safe.

*From the right forward a small gang of Negroes enter. They are
dressed in striped convict suits, their heads are shaven, one leg drags
limpingly, shackled to a heavy ball and chain. Some carry picks, the
others shovels. They are followed by a white man dressed in the uniform
of a PRISON GUARD. A Winchester rifle is slung across his
shoulders and he carries a heavy whip. At a signal from the guard they
stop on the road opposite where JONES is sitting. JONES, who has
been staring up at the sky, unmindful of their noiseless approach,
suddenly looks down and sees them. His eyes pop out, he tries to get to
his feet and fly, but sinks back, too numbed by fright to move. His voice
catches in a choking prayer.*

JONES. Lawd Jesus!

*The PRISON GUARD cracks his whip – noiselessly and at that
signal all the CONVICTS start at work on the road. They swing their
picks, they shovel, but not a sound comes from their labour. Their
movements, like those of JEFF in the preceding scene, are those of
automatons – rigid, slow, and mechanical. The PRISON GUARD
points sternly at JONES with his whip, motions him to take his place
among the other shovellers. JONES gets to his feet in a hypnotized
stupor. He mumbles subserviently.*

JONES. Yes, suh! Yes, suh! I'se comin'.

As he shuffles, dragging one foot, over to his place, he curses under his breath with rage and hatred.

God damn yo' soul, I gits even wid you yit, some time.

As if there were a shovel in his hands he goes through weary, mechanical gestures of digging up dirt, and throwing it to the roadside. Suddenly the GUARD *approaches him angrily, threateningly. He raises his whip and lashes* JONES *viciously across the shoulders with it.* JONES *winces with pain and cowers abjectly. The* GUARD *turns his back on him and walks away contemptuously. Instantly* JONES *straightens up. With arms upraised as if his shovel were a club in his hands he springs murderously at the unsuspecting guard. In the act of crashing down his shovel on the white man's skull,* JONES *suddenly becomes aware that his hands are empty. He cries despairingly.*

Whar's my shovel? Gimme my shovel 'till I splits his damn head! (*Appealing to his fellow* CONVICTS.) Gimme a shovel one o' you, fo' God's sake!

They stand fixed in motionless attitudes, their eyes on the ground. The GUARD *seems to wait expectantly, his back turned to the attacker.* JONES *bellows with baffled, terrified rage, tugging frantically at his revolver.*

I kills you, you white debil, if it's de last thing I evah does! Ghost or debil, I kill you agin!

He frees the revolver and fires point blank at the GUARD's *back. Instantly the walls of the forest close in from both sides, the road and the figures of the* CONVICT GANG *are blotted out in an enshrouding darkness. The only sounds are a crashing in the underbrush as* JONES *leaps away in mad flight and the throbbing of the tom-tom, still far distant, but increased in volume of sound and rapidity of beat.*

Scene Five

One o'clock. A large circular clearing, enclosed by the serried ranks of gigantic trunks of tall trees whose tops are lost to view. In the centre is a big dead stump worn by time into a curious resemblance to an auction block. The moon floods the clearing with a clear light.

JONES *forces his way through the forest on the left. He looks wildly*

*about the clearing with hunted, fearful glances. His trousers are in
tatters, his shoes cut and misshapen, flapping about his feet. He slinks
cautiously to the stump in the centre and sits down in a tense position,
ready for instant flight. Then he holds his head in his hands and rocks
back and forth, moaning to himself miserably.*

JONES. Oh Lawd, Lawd! Oh Lawd, Lawd! (*Suddenly he throws
himself on his knees and raises his clasped hands to the sky – in a voice
of agonized pleading.*) Lawd Jesus, heah my prayer! I'se a po'
sinner, a po' sinner! I knows I done wrong, I knows it! When I
cotches Jeff cheatin' wid loaded dice my anger overcomes me
and I kills him dead! Lawd, I done wrong! When dat guard
hits me wid de whip, my anger overcomes me, and I kills him
dead. Lawd, I done wrong! And down heah whar dese fool
bush niggers raises me up to the seat o' de mighty, I steals all I
could grab. Lawd, I done wrong! I knows it! I'se sorry! Forgive
me, Lawd! Forgive dis po' sinner! (*Then beseeching terrifiedly.*)
And keep dem away, Lawd! Keep dem away from me! And
stop dat drum soundin' in my ears! Dat begin to sound ha'nted,
too. (*He gets to his feet, evidently slightly reassured by his prayer –
with attempted confidence.*) De Lawd'll preserve me from dem
ha'nts after dis. (*Sits down on the stump again.*) I ain't skeered o'
real men. Let dem come. But dem odders – (*He shudders – then
looks down at his feet, working his toes inside the shoes – with a
groan.*) Oh, my po' feet! Dem shoes ain't no use no more
'ceptin' to hurt. I'se better off widout dem. (*He unlaces them and
pulls them off – holds the wrecks of the shoes in his hands and regards
them mournfully.*) You was real, A-one patin' leather, too. Look
at you now. Emperor, you'se gittin' mighty low!

*He sighs dejectedly and remains with bowed shoulders, staring down at
the shoes in his hands as if reluctant to throw them away. While his
attention is thus occupied, a crowd of figures silently enter the clearing
from all sides. All are dressed in Southern costumes of the period of the
fifties of the last century. There are middle-aged men who are evidently
well-to-do* PLANTERS. *There is one spruce, authoritative individual
– the* AUCTIONEER. *There are a crowd of curious spectators,
chiefly young belles and dandies who have come to the slave-market for
diversion. All exchange courtly greetings in dumb show and chat
silently together. There is something stiff, rigid, unreal, marionettish
about their movements. They group themselves about the stump. Finally
a batch of slaves are led in from the left by an attendant – three men of
different ages, two women, one with a baby in her arms, nursing. They
are placed to the left of the stump, beside* JONES.

The WHITE PLANTERS *look them over appraisingly as if they were cattle. The dandies point their fingers and make witty remarks. The belles titter bewitchingly. All this in silence save for the ominous throb of the tom-tom. The* AUCTIONEER *holds up his hand, taking his place at the stump. The groups strain forward. He touches* JONES *on the shoulder peremptorily, motioning for him to stand on the stump – the auction block.*

JONES *looks up, sees the figures on all sides, looks wildly for some opening to escape, sees none, screams, and leaps madly to the top of the stump to get as far away from them as possible. He stands there, cowering, paralysed with horror. The* AUCTIONEER *begins his silent speech. He points to* JONES, *appeals to the planters to see for themselves. Here is a good field hand, sound in wind and limb as they can see. Very strong still in spite of his being middle-aged. Look at that back. Look at those shoulders. Look at the muscles in his arms and his sturdy legs. Capable of any amount of hard labour. Moreover of a good disposition, intelligent and tractable. Will any gentleman start the bidding? The planters raise their fingers, make their bids. They are apparently all eager to possess* JONES. *The bidding is lively, the crowd interested. While this has been going on,* JONES *has been seized by the courage of desperation. He dares to look down and around him. Over his face abject terror gives way to mystification, to gradual realization – stutteringly.*

JONES. What you all doin', white folks? What's all dis? What you all lookin' at me fo'? What you doin' wid me, anyhow? (*Suddenly convulsed with raging hatred and fear.*) Is dis a auction? Is you sellin' me like dey uster befo' de war? (*Jerking out his revolver just as the* AUCTIONEER *knocks him down to one of the planters, glaring from him to the purchaser.*) And you sells me? And you buys me? I shows you I'se a free nigger, damn yo' souls!

He fires at the AUCTIONEER *and at the* PLANTER *with such rapidity that the two shots are almost simultaneous. As if this were a signal the walls of the forest fold in. Only blackness remains and silence broken by* JONES *as he rushes off, crying with fear – and by the quickened, ever louder beat of the tom-tom.*

Scene Six

Three o'clock. A cleared space in the forest. The limbs of the trees meet over it forming a low ceiling about five feet from the ground. The interlocked ropes of creepers reaching upward to entwine the tree trunks give an arched appearance to the sides. The space thus enclosed is like the dark, noisome hold of some ancient vessel. The moonlight is almost completely shut out and only a vague, wan light filters through.

There is the noise of someone approaching from the left, stumbling and crawling through the undergrowth. JONES's voice is heard between chattering moans.

JONES. Oh, Lawd, what I gwine do now? Ain't got no bullet left on'y de silver one. If mo' o' dem ha'nts come after me, how I gwine skeer dem away? Oh, Lawd, on'y de silver one left – an' I gotta save dat fo' luck. If I shoots dat one I'm a goner sho'! Lawd, it's black heah! Whar's de moon? Oh, Lawd, don't dis night evah come to an end? (*By the sounds, he is feeling his way cautiously forward.*) Dere! Dis feels like a clear space. I gotta lie down an' rest. I don't care if dem niggers does cotch me. I gotta rest.

He is well forward now where his figure can be dimly made out. His trousers have been so torn away that what is left of them is no better than a loin-cloth. He flings himself full length, face downward on the ground, panting with exhaustion. Gradually it seems to grow lighter in the enclosed space and two rows of seated figures can be seen behind JONES. They are sitting in crumpled, despairing attitudes, hunched, facing one another with their backs touching the forest walls as if they were shackled to them. All are Negroes naked save for loin-cloths. At first they are silent and motionless. Then they begin to sway slowly forward toward each and back in unison, as if they were laxly letting themselves follow the long roll of a ship at sea. At the same time a low, melancholy murmur rises among them, increasing gradually by rhythmic degrees which seem to be directed and controlled by the throb of the tom-tom in the distance, to a long, tremulous wail of despair that reaches a certain pitch, unbearably acute, then falls by slow gradations of tone into silence and is taken up again. JONES starts, looks up, sees the figures, and throws himself down again to shut out the sight. A shudder of terror shakes his whole body as the wail rises up about him again. But the next time his voice, as if under some uncanny compulsion, starts with the others. As their chorus lifts he rises to a sitting posture similar to the others, swaying back and forth. His voice reaches the highest pitch of sorrow, of desolation. The light fades out, the other voices cease, and only darkness is left. JONES can be heard scrambling to his feet and running off, his voice sinking down the scale and receding as he moves farther and farther away in the forest. The tom-tom beats louder, quicker, with a more insistent, triumphant pulsation.

Scene Seven

Five o'clock. The foot of a gigantic tree by the edge of a great river. A rough structure of boulders, like an altar, is by the tree. The raised river bank is in the nearer background. Beyond this the surface of the river spreads out, brilliant and unruffled in the moonlight, blotted out and merged in a veil of bluish mist in the distance.

JONES's voice is heard from the left rising and falling in the long, despairing wail of the chained slaves, to the rhythmic beat of the tom-tom. As his voice sinks into silence, he enters the open space. The expression of his face is fixed and stony, his eyes have an obsessed glare, he moves with a strange deliberation like a sleep-walker or one in a trance. He looks around at the tree, the rough stone altar, the moonlit surface of the river beyond, and passes his hand over his head with a vague gesture of puzzled bewilderment. Then, as if in obedience to some obscure impulse, he sinks into a kneeling, devotional posture before the altar. Then he seems to come to himself partly, to have an uncertain realization of what he is doing, for he straightens up and stares about him horrifiedly – in an incoherent mumble.

JONES. What – what is I doin'? What is – dis place? Seems like – seems like I know dat tree – an' dem stones – an' de river. I remember – seems like I been heah befo'. (*Tremblingly.*) Oh, Gorry, I'se skeered in dis place! I'se skeered! Oh, Lawd, pertect dis sinner!

Crawling away from the altar, he cowers close to the ground, his face hidden, his shoulders heaving with sobs of hysterical fright. From behind the trunk of the tree, as if he had sprung out of it, the figure of the Congo WITCH-DOCTOR appears. He is wizened and old, naked except for the fur of some small animal tied about his waist, its bushy tail hanging down in front. His body is stained all over a bright red. Antelope horns are on each side of his head, branching upward. In one hand he carries a bone rattle, in the other a charm stick with a bunch of white cockatoo feathers tied to the end. A great number of glass beads and bone ornaments are about his neck, ears, wrists, and ankles. He struts noiselessly with a queer prancing step to a position in the clear ground between JONES and the altar. Then with a preliminary, summoning stamp of his foot on the earth, he begins to dance and to chant. As if in response to his summons the beating of the tom-tom grows to a fierce, exultant boom whose throbs seem to fill the air with vibrating rhythm. JONES looks up, starts to spring to his feet, reaches a half-kneeling, half-squatting position and remains rigidly fixed there, paralysed with awed fascination by this new apparition. The WITCH-DOCTOR sways, stamping with his foot, his bone rattle clicking the time. His voice rises and falls in a weird, monotonous croon, without articulate word divisions. Gradually his dance becomes clearly one of a narrative in pantomime, his croon is an incantation, a charm to allay the fierceness of some implacable deity demanding sacrifice. He flees, he is pursued by devils, he hides, he flees again. Ever wilder and wilder becomes his flight, nearer and nearer draws the pursuing evil, more and more the spirit of terror gains possession of him. His croon, rising to intensity, is punctuated by shrill cries. JONES *has become completely hypnotized. His voice joins in the incantation, in the cries, he beats time with his hands and sways his body to and fro from the waist. The whole spirit and meaning of the dance has entered into him, has become his spirit. Finally the theme of the pantomime halts on a howl of despair, and is taken up again in a note of savage hope. There is a salvation. The forces of evil demand sacrifice. They must be appeased. The* WITCH-DOCTOR *points with his wand to the sacred tree, to the river beyond, to the altar, and finally to* JONES *with a ferocious command.* JONES *seems to sense the meaning of this. It is he who must offer himself for sacrifice. He beats his forehead abjectly to the ground, moaning hysterically.*

JONES. Mercy, oh Lawd! Mercy! Mercy on dis po' sinner.

The WITCH-DOCTOR *springs to the river bank. He stretches out his arms and calls to some god within its depths. Then he starts backward slowly, his arms remaining out. A huge head of a crocodile appears over the bank and its eyes, glittering greenly, fasten upon* JONES. *He stares into them fascinatedly. The* WITCH-DOCTOR *prances up to him, touches him with his wand, motions with hideous command towards the waiting monster.* JONES *squirms on his belly nearer and nearer, moaning continually.*

JONES. Mercy, Lawd! Mercy!

The crocodile heaves more of his enormous hulk on to the land. JONES *squirms toward him. The* WITCH-DOCTOR's *voice shrills out in furious exultation, the tom-tom beats madly.* JONES *cries out in a fierce, exhausted spasm of anguished pleading.*

JONES. Lawd, save me! Lawd Jesus, heah my prayer!

Immediately, in answer to his prayer, comes the thought of the one bullet left him. He snatches at his hip, shouting defiantly.

De silver bullet! You don't git me yit!

He fires at the green eyes in front of him. The head of the crocodile sinks back behind the river bank, the WITCH-DOCTOR *springs behind the sacred tree and disappears.* JONES *lies with his face to the ground, his arms outstretched, whimpering with fear as the throb of the tom-tom fills the silence about him with a sombre pulsation, a baffled but revengeful power.*

Scene Eight

Dawn. Same as Scene Two, the dividing line of forest and plain. The nearest tree trunks are dimly revealed, but the forest behind them is still a mass of glooming shadow. The tom-tom seems on the very spot, so loud and continuously vibrating are its beats.

LEM *enters from the left, followed by a small squad of his* SOLDIERS, *and by the Cockney trader,* SMITHERS. LEM *is a heavy-set, ape-faced old savage of the extreme African type, dressed only in a loin-cloth. A revolver and cartridge belt are about his waist. His* SOLDIERS *are in different degrees of rag-concealed nakedness. All wear broad palm-leaf hats. Each one carries a rifle.* SMITHERS *is the same as in Scene One. One of the soldiers, evidently a tracker, is peering about keenly on the ground. He grunts and points to the spot where* JONES *entered the forest.* LEM *and* SMITHERS *come to look.*

SMITHERS *(after a glance, turns away in disgust).* That's where 'e went in right enough. Much good it'll do yer. 'E's miles orf by this an' safe to the coast, damn 's 'ide! I tole yer yer'd lose 'im, didn't I? – wastin' the 'ole bloomin' night beatin' yer bloody drum and castin' yer silly spells! Gawd blimey, wot a pack!

LEM *(gutturally).* We cotch him. You see. *(He makes a motion to his soldiers who squat down on their haunches in a semi-circle.)*

SMITHERS *(exasperatedly).* Well, ain't yer goin' in an' 'unt 'im in the woods? What the 'ell's the good of waitin'?

LEM *(imperturbably – squatting down himself).* We cotch him.

SMITHERS *(turning away from him contemptuously).* Aw! Garn! 'E's a better man than the lot o' you put together. I 'ates the sight o' 'im, but I'll say that for 'im.

A sound of snapping twigs comes from the forest. The SOLDIERS *jump to their feet, cocking their rifles alertly.* LEM *remains sitting with an imperturbable expression, but listening intently. The sound from the woods is repeated.* LEM *makes a quick signal with his hands. His followers creep quickly but noiselessly into the forest, scattering so that each enters at a different spot.*

SMITHERS *(in the silence that follows – in a contemptuous whisper).* You ain't thinkin' that would be 'im, I 'ope?

LEM (*calmly*). We cotch him.

SMITHERS. Blarsted fat 'eads! (*Then after a second's thought –
wonderingly.*) Still, after all, it might 'appen. If 'e lost 'is bloody way
in these stinkin' woods 'e'd likely turn in a circle without 'is
knowin' it. They all does.

LEM (*peremptorily*). Ssshh! (*The reports of several rifles sound from the
forest, followed a second later by savage, exultant yells. The beating of the
tom-tom abruptly ceases. LEM looks up at the white man with a grin of
satisfaction.*) We cotch him. Him dead.

SMITHERS (*with a snarl*). 'Ow d'yer know it's 'im, an' 'ow d'yer
know 'e's dead?

LEM. My mens dey got 'um silver bullets. Dey kill him shure.

SMITHERS (*astonished*). They got silver bullets?

LEM. Lead bullet no kill him. He got um strong charm. I cook um
money, make um silver bullet, make um strong charm, too.

SMITHERS (*light breaking upon him*). So that's wot you was up to all
night, wot? You was scared to put after 'im till you'd moulded
silver bullets, eh?

LEM (*simply stating a fact*). Yes. Him got strong charm. Lead no good.

SMITHERS (*slapping his thigh and guffawing*). Haw-haw! If yer don't
beat all 'ell! (*Then recovering himself – scornfully.*) I'll bet yer it ain't
'im they shot at all, yer bleedin' looney!

LEM (*calmly*). Dey come bring him now. (*The SOLDIERS come out of
the forest, carrying JONES's limp body. There is a little reddish-purple
hole under his left breast. He is dead. They carry him to LEM, who
examines his body with great satisfaction.*)

SMITHERS (*leans over his shoulder – in a tone of frightened awe*). Well,
they did for yer right enough, Jonesy, me lad! Dead as a bloater!
(*Mockingly.*) Where's yer 'igh an' mighty airs now, yer bloomin'
Majesty? (*Then with a grin.*) Silver bullets! Gawd blimey, but yer
died in the 'eight o' style, any'ow! (*LEM makes a motion to the
soldiers to carry the body out, left. SMITHERS speaks to him sneeringly.*)
And I s'pose you think it's yer bleedin' charms and yer silly
beatin' the drum that made 'im run in a circle when 'e'd lost
'imself, don't yer? (*But LEM makes no reply, does not seem to hear the
question, walks out, left, after his men. SMITHERS looks after him with
contemptuous scorn.*) Stupid as 'ogs, the lot of 'em! Blarsted niggers!

The curtain falls.